The Future
of the Christian

THE
FUTURE
OF THE
CHRISTIAN

ELTON TRUEBLOOD

PROFESSOR AT LARGE

EARLHAM COLLEGE

1817

HARPER & ROW, PUBLISHERS

NEW YORK, EVANSTON, AND LONDON

LIBRARY OF CONGRESS CATALOG CARD NUMBER: 70-126281

FOR VIRGINIA
Who shares my hopes

Preface

ONE OF THE most exciting ideas that has ever entered my mind is that we are living in the early days of the Christian faith. We are early Christians! What is supremely fortunate is that the faith which sustains us has not become rigid. The stability of the central conviction has been shown to be compatible with flexibility of application. There is abundant reason to believe that there will be a Christian future, since it is evident that God has purposes for this world which are not yet fulfilled and that men can be His instruments in working for their fulfillment. If, as is probable, we shall have descendants thousands of years hence, they may look back upon us as living much closer to the beginning of the faith than to its end, and the strong likelihood is that they will be right. It is our opportunity, not merely to restore the Christian faith, and not merely to maintain it, but to guide it into new channels.

This volume, which is inspired primarily by the idea just mentioned, is intended as part of a literary continuum which began in 1944, with the publication of *The Predicament of Modern Man.* The format of that book was adopted deliberately in the conscious hope of reaching the ordinary thoughtful reader, the purpose determining both size and style. It was my conviction, when I wrote my first book of this character in the dark days of the war, that serious thinking can be presented with clarity, providing the author is willing to engage in the discipline requisite to his task.

The selection of a title is never easy, but the naming of the present book has been particularly difficult. At one time the expectation was to call it "Early Christians," but it was soon realized that potential readers might suppose that a book bearing this title was devoted to ancient history. What was required was a title which would make it clear that all of the thinking expressed in the book concerns the future. Thoughtful people are concerned with the future because that is the only area of experience about which anything can be done. We cannot change the past, and the present is gone as soon as it is reported, but the future is that in which we can make a difference.

Prediction is seldom successful, not merely because finite beings are ignorant, but, even more, because the future is fundamentally indeterminate. The future of mankind, far from being something already fixed, is undecided, and it is undecided for the important reason that men are free. Because we live in an open universe, we are always involved in the paradox that the future, which cannot be fully foreseen, provides the one opportunity for human beings to produce change. By thinking, the future is altered! The practical possibility of such alteration in the character of the Christian Cause arises from the fact that, though we possess an unchanging truth, the truth requires continually fresh articulation and demonstration. While we cannot know with certainty what the Christianity of the future will be, it is possible to have some intimations of the general direction which it must take if it is to be true to its fundamental genius.

D.E.T.

Earlham College
Labor Day, 1970

I

THE MIRACLE
OF SURVIVAL

*The lamp the Lord has lighted is not utterly
extinct.*

IS OURS "the post-Christian age"? It is clear that many
observers think so. They believe that we live, or are
about to live, in a civilization in which the Christian religion has historical interest, but no more. The question
whether the Christian has any future is being asked with
all seriousness, particularly by people who think the answer is negative. The sober conclusion which they have
reached is that, though the Christian faith has long been
influential in the life of the West, its day of spiritual domi-
nance is over. The Biblical conception of life and truth,
which served adequately in simpler or less sophisticated
periods of human history, has now, many are convinced,
ceased to be either intellectually acceptable or culturally

powerful. It has, they believe, at last run its course and will soon, therefore, be extinct.

A related question is whether there will be any future for anybody. Though the conviction seldom reaches the level of cogent expression, it appears that some are willing to settle for temporary living because they doubt that there will be a human future of any kind. What they mean is that they think the human race will not be able to survive very long, in view of the tensions, pollutions, and antagonisms which have surfaced or are about to surface. They think that we are literally at the end of the age.

Those who believe that there will be a future, but not a Christian future, consider that Christianity is in the same general position in which the religions of ancient Greece stood when the Apostle Paul and his little team of Christians visited Mars Hill about 50 A.D. At that time there were still numerous physical evidences of the once powerful faith, including what some consider the world's most beautiful building, but the meaning had departed. Shrines were abundantly evident (Acts 17:23), but already their chief significance was that of antiques.

That the Judeo-Christian faith has produced many monuments which endure is something which nobody doubts or denies; what is denied is contemporary significance. The widely expressed idea is that the intellectual bankruptcy of organized religion is so patent that only those who are blinded by professional bias can fail to see it. Millions are convinced that what now goes on in organized religion could cease without loss or harm, in any important way, to the patterns of ordinary life. Even conscientious objection to participation in war is now legally recognized, wholly without reference to religious belief or practices, either singly or in groups. In numerous academic centers religion is no longer opposed; it is simply ignored. In some of the very colleges which were founded

by Christian conviction and sacrifice, the popular conviction, on the part of both students and instructors, is that
Christianity, whatever it may have accomplished in the
past, has very little present significance and has ultimately
no future at all. Out of seven instructors in one important
philosophy department, only one considers himself a
Christian. Some thoughtful observers naturally conclude
that the end of the Christian faith has come. Since the
evidence which influences their judgment is genuine,
though it is not the only evidence, we must take a harder
look at the question.

The most convincing way of challenging the assumption of the inevitable extinction of the Christian Cause is
to center our attention, not upon speculation, but upon
historical fact. The survival of the Christian faith, along
with its Hebraic roots, is one of the most revealing facts of
all human history, because the survival has occurred
against incredible odds. At first there was a tiny band,
whose Leader had been executed as a criminal. When they
said He had risen, most people disbelieved them. They had
neither money nor prestige nor political influence. It is
easy to forget that, in the beginning, nearly all of the
secular forces were antagonistic to early Christianity. That
the Stoic and Epicurean philosophers were contemptuous
is shown by their famous question, "What can this charla-
tan be trying to say?" (Acts 17:18, *New English Bible*). It is
part of the stunning paradox of history, however, that the
time came when the schools of both condescending groups
had ceased to exist, while the despised group continued,
not only to exist, but to grow.

That the group gathered in the name of the risen Christ
would soon disappear was the natural expectation of outside observers, though one of them, Gamaliel, was astute
enough to recognize that the new movement might prove
to be an exception to the general rule. Enthusiastic move-

ments, the scholar recognized, tend to be short-lived, but this one might prove to be different. "If it is of God," said Gamaliel with penetrating accuracy, "you will not be able to overthrow them" (Acts 5:39).[1] That Gamaliel's outside guess was correct is supported by the accumulation of historical evidence, not merely in regard to the early stages, but to succeeding centuries of Christian experience as well. When the Roman Empire, which provided such fierce persecution, itself came to an end, the persecuted fellowship went right on living and has never ended to this day.

Much of Christian history has been a series of verifications of the truth of the Apostle's words when he wrote that "a great opportunity has opened for effective work, and there is much opposition" (I Cor. 16:9, NEB). Though Paul was referring specifically to the situation in Ephesus, his words have continuing validity and are highly pertinent at the present time. Always there has been the paradox that opposition and opportunity tend to go hand in hand.

The historical examples which demonstrate the way in which Christian vitality has appeared in response to danger are so numerous that it is difficult to know where to start in enumerating them. One of the most vivid examples is that of the early Quaker Movement from 1650 to 1690. During that period there was fierce persecution, not only in the British Isles, but also in the English colonies on the American seacoast. In Aberdeen, Scotland, the Tolbooth prison was jammed with Quakers during the long cold winter of 1676-1677. In Boston four, including one woman, were hanged. Sometimes, with nearly all of the adult members imprisoned, the children gathered regularly without their parents. What is extremely impressive

1. Scripture quotations are from the Revised Standard Version, unless otherwise indicated.

is that the vitality continued for forty years, and then declined visibly when acceptance of the despised people became general.

When we consider the endurance of the Christian faith, it is not unreasonable to call it a miracle. Not only has there been fierce opposition and contempt from the outside; there has, at the same time, been corruption and incompetence on the inside. Even the marvelous Letters to the Christians at Corinth, which contain some of the finest prose in any language, were written because of the very ineptitude of the early Church. Paul wrote eloquently of love, chiefly because it was so obviously lacking. Already there was bickering and struggle for power, yet the movement survived, to serve as leaven in the pagan culture. The faith continued, not because of the perfection of Christians, but in spite of their imperfections. It is hard to avoid the conclusion that the Church is the result of God's doing, since neither attacks from the outside nor human sin and foolishness on the inside has been able to kill it in the past. We are driven back in reverence to the prediction of Christ, when He first mentioned the Church. "The forces of death," He said, "shall never overpower it" (Matt. 16:18, NEB).

The majesty of Christ's prediction, and its fulfillment, is increasingly impressed upon our minds when we think of the numerous dangers of the different centuries. We rejoice that our American form of government has survived without a break, and without a violent take-over, for more than one hundred eighty years, but this pales into relative insignificance when we contemplate the fact that the Christian faith has existed for more than ten times as long. If we think of the entire Biblical faith as a unit, including both the Hebraic and the Christian, we soon realize that we are dealing with the most enduring fellowship in all the world. The remarkable way in which the Hebrew Scriptures have become essential elements in Christian consciousness justifies reference to continuity. In an important sense, the movement which started with Abraham, and which expanded into Christianity, is actually one movement.

How could the faith have endured through the Dark Ages when much of both science and general learning was lost? How could the faith have endured the break between the East and the West, and the even more damaging break, in the sixteenth century, within the Western Church? The tensions arising from the emergence of modern natural science, the challenges of the enlightenment, and the violent attacks involved in the ideology of the French Revolution are all part of one story, the story of miraculous survival. Even the fierce persecution within the Church, driving Huguenots from France, Puritans from England, and extreme Protestants from the Rhineland, served mightily to provide human assets to the New World and eventually to strengthen the Church.

There is a curious naïveté about supposing that a faith which has been able to endure in the face of so many and varied difficulties will, because of the particular difficulties which the contemporary world is able to present, succumb now. To assume that contemporary paganism can succeed in a task in which the worst of Roman emperors and the most corrupt of Popes failed, is to take ourselves altogether too seriously. The best reason to conclude that the Christian faith will survive the challenges of our generation is that it *has* survived far harder challenges, not for a short period, but for centuries.

It is important for the contemporary Christian to realize that the expectation of the death of the Christian Movement is no new phenomenon. This is not the first generation in which demise has been confidently predicted, but the predictions have always failed to materialize. It is very likely that our successors will note, not the differences between the Christianity of the end of the twentieth century and that of earlier periods, but rather the fundamental similarity. We are not, it is true, persecuted bodily, as were Christians in the days of Nero, and we are not hounded out of our country as were the Huguenots and Mennonites, but we are daily subjected to intellectual condescension. There is a beneficent aspect to the fact that the upholders of the faith are always cast in the role of those who must fight for its survival. One result is that Christians become less vulnerable to the temptation to complacency.

The major secret of survival is the recurrent phenomenon of renewal on the inside. Over and over, when death appears to be inevitable, new life emerges, not because of some outside influence, but because of the energy of an inner vitality. That this theme belongs to the entire Judeo-Christian heritage, rather than to Christianity alone, is made clear by reference to the most famous parable of the Hebrew Scriptures, the parable of the Valley of Dry Bones (Ezek. 37:1-14). The parable begins with the description of dry bones in the valley, where, presumably in consequence of a battle, the bones are completely dried, presenting no evidence of life at all. The miracle is that, as the prophet watches, the dry bones come together; they are joined by sinews; and they are covered with skin. Finally, breath enters into them and they live! This resurrection, we are told, is a parable of the vitality of God's people which is never entirely lost, however discouraging the situation may appear to be. The prophet hears: "Son of man, these bones are the whole house of Israel. Behold, they say, 'Our bones are dried up, and our hope is lost; we are clean cut off.' Therefore prophesy, and say to them, Thus says the Lord God: 'Behold, I will open your graves, and raise you from your graves, O my people' " (37:11, 12).

The lesson of the emergence of life from dry bones has

been illustrated in actual history again and again. Just when deadness has seemed to be complete, freshness has emerged in the most unexpected places. Who could have predicted the amazing burst which appeared in the vicinity of Assisi near the beginning of the thirteenth century? The instrument of renewal, whom we call St. Francis, was not even a theologian, but a modest ex-soldier. We are deeply indebted to Stephen Neill for the clarity with which he has described the recurring pattern of the self-renewal of the faith. "History shows us again and again," he writes, "that, when everything seemed at its darkest, God has in the most unexpected way caused new light to shine in the darkness. With the advantage of hindsight, we can see a long process of preparation for the Reformation through the Middle Ages; yet the most optimistic prophet of reform in those times could hardly have foreseen the emergence of Martin Luther on the horizon of world history."[2]

The study of history does many things for us, but one of its greatest benefits is that it is an antidote to quick judgment. History undermines both complacency and pessimism. The more we study our historical lesson, the more our mood is a combination of both realism and expectancy. There is always a chance that we shall decline, but likewise, there is an equal chance that new light will break forth.

The Christian who needs encouragement is well advised to study the eighteenth century as much as he can. In the early part of that century, especially in England, the Christian faith appeared to be at one of its lowest points, much of the discouragement being also reflected in the mood of the English colonists of America. The "Century of Genius" seemed far in the past, while the gigantic influence of Samuel Johnson in England and of John Woolman in America had not yet emerged. There were no powerful

2. Stephen Neill, *Call to Mission* (Philadelphia: Fortress Press, 1970), p. 89.

Christian voices such as those of John Milton, George Fox, Jeremy Taylor, and Richard Baxter to arouse people as they had been aroused in the middle of the seventeenth century. The noble Joseph Butler, who seemed almost alone, gave vivid expression to the dominant mood which he proposed to challenge. "It is come, I know not how," he wrote in 1736, "to be taken for granted, by many persons, that Christianity is not so much as a subject of inquiry; but that it is, now at length, discovered to be fictitious. Accordingly they treat it as if, in the present age, this were an agreed point among all people of discernment; and nothing remained, but to set it up as a principal subject of mirth and ridicule, as it were by way of reprisals, for its having so long interrupted the pleasures of the world."[3]

Because there are features which the twentieth century and the eighteenth century have in common, Bishop Butler's words have genuine contemporary applicability. What is most striking about his words, however, is the rapidity with which they were made obsolete by events in the same century. Even as they were written, John Wesley was already thirty-three years of age and on the threshold of his remarkable influence which changed the general climate of opinion in both Britain and America. Though Joseph Butler described accurately the mood of his day as he began to write, he was naturally not able to envisage, at that time, the radical change in mood that was about to appear.

The only way for a Christian to be loyal to his central commitment is to be as honest as he knows how to be. It is important to survive, but it is even more important to tell the truth, and we can never tell the truth if we are seeking, primarily, to prove a point. The fact of survival in a stormy past is highly instructive, and must give pause to any who

3. Joseph Butler, *The Analogy of Religion* (Philadelphia: J. B. Lippincott Co., 1900), p. 66.

refer, with bland confidence, to the demise of the Christian faith, but the Christian must also be warned against a bland optimism.

What is most significant, moreover, is that the honest facing of the darkness is one of the chief evidences of the brightness. A sign of strength in the Christian Movement today is that its representatives are willing to admit, without embarrassment, the serious difficulties of their situation. In Professor Bellah's striking phrase, we are moving from "the loss of faith" to "the faith of loss," which, he explains, "is closer to joy than to despair."[4]

The strongest contemporary criticisms of the Christian faith, as it is actually demonstrated today, come not from outside antagonists, but from insiders who are sad at what they see and consequently seek to change it. In practically no instances are contemporary Christians complacent. What saddens them most of all is the sharp division which weakens the forces of Christ in the world. Reference is not hereby made to the existence of separate denominations or to the rift which occurred when Roman Catholics and Protestants divided more than four hundred years ago. Indeed, one sign of contemporary renewal is the degree to which Roman Catholics and Protestants can now walk together in harmony. The Roman Catholic official hymn book includes Martin Luther's "A Mighty Fortress Is Our God" and some of the hymns written by Charles Wesley. In a similar way Protestants now employ details of Catholic liturgy.

The serious division, which makes Christians weep, is within denominations, and even within individual congregations, when the members separate into competing parties. Often each group stresses one part of what is meant to be a total gospel, on the strange assumption that emphasis on one side requires neglect of another. The sharpest

4. Robert N. Bellah, *Beyond Belief* (New York: Harper & Row, 1970), p. xxi.

cleavage now exists between those who give their major attention to social action and those who emphasize the inner life of devotion.

Whenever the faith is thus separated the result is always tragic, for the merely fractional is not worthy of survival. It would be hard to defend the worth of a faith, for example, in which people rejoice in their own personal salvation while they pay little or no attention to the economic and racial injustices about them. But it is equally tragic to witness what is really the greater danger at this period of our history, the development of social action divorced from any cultivation of either reverence or humility. Though social action is a necessary feature of the Christian life, it cannot long be sustained if it is social action and only that. It is the clear teaching of Christ that men are to be known by their fruits, which may be understood partly as acts of compassion and justice, but it is sometimes forgotten that Christ was also concerned with the danger represented by *temporary* fruits. The flashy event which catches the headlines is never adequate, because endurance is required. The lesson of history is that, if it is not to wither, the social conscience requires steady nourishment in a deep religious experience. Here the words of the parable of the seeds and soils are specific and clear: "When the sun rose the young corn was scorched, and as it had no proper root it withered away" (Mark 4:6, NEB). The same theme appears in the Fourth Gospel where Christ's expressed interest is not merely in fruit, but in "fruit that shall last" (John 15:16, NEB).

The obvious truth is that more than one emphasis is necessary. As though sensing this danger in advance, Christ said: "It is these you should have practised, without neglecting the others" (Luke 11:42, NEB). There is no necessary conflict between being a doer and a believer. Nobody really supposes that the action of repeating a creed is sufficient to make a person a Christian, but the recognition that the creed is insufficient has led, by a curious logic, to the absurd conclusion that the creed is *unnecessary*. What is therefore required is a tough-minded rationality concerning the necessary and the sufficient. Unless we understand clearly that what a man believes determines in large measure what he does, all our talk about renewal will become worthless.

The plight of the theological seminaries is so serious that it is difficult to exaggerate it. In some of them the blight of anti-intellectualism is so extreme that some sections of the libraries are virtually deserted. We seem to be producing amateur psychologists and sociologists who would find it impossible to defend intelligently a Christian world view. Worse still, many now hold that such an intellectual operation is unnecessary. It is not very surprising, therefore, that, in Milton's phrase, the hungry sheep look up and are not fed. It would help our generation to remember the warning of Professor Whitehead when he said, "Mere ritual and emotion cannot maintain themselves untouched by intellectuality."[5]

Some of the academic theology which we do have tends to be little more than a succession of fads. Because it is so obviously dated now, it is hard even to believe that only a few years ago, some theological professors were taking seriously the idea that thoughtful people could be committed to Christ and yet not believe in the Living God. The general public was less naïve, many a humble follower of Christ being able to see, without professional assistance, that the idea of Christian atheism is a prime example of self-contradiction. If God is not, then Christ was wrong, and if He was wrong at the central point, why should we pay attention to Him at any other?

In spite of glorious exceptions, for which we are deeply

5. Alfred North Whitehead, *Religion in the Making* (New York: The Macmillan Company, 1926), p. 23.

thankful, there is evident lack of vitality in the Christian community. The decline in attendance at public worship, though such worship is by no means the only item of importance in the expression of the faith, is one indication of general weakness. If this decline were balanced by new vitality in some other area, we might take heart, but often this vitality is not apparent. It is obvious to any impartial observer that the worst decline is appearing in the affluent churches, and that the most violent separation from Christian roots in colleges appears in the academic institutions which are the most prestigious. It is, indeed, very hard for the affluent to "enter the kingdom of God" (Luke 18:24). But part of the Good News is that, though entrance is very hard, it is not, for that reason, impossible. Few sentences are more reassuring, when all seems to be dark and hopeless, than the words of Christ when He said, "With God all things are possible" (Matt. 19:26).

Though it is always difficult to know, in any accurate sense, what time it is, it is the Christian's duty to be aware of where we are and whither we are tending (Luke 12:56). Some have cited interest in esoteric religions as a sign of hope, but it is by no means self-evident that this is a true interpretation of the facts. Study of Oriental religions and the emergence of quasi-religious forms of humanism are important, but their chief importance is that they show that spiritual needs, not met in one way, will be met in another. It is emptiness that cannot endure.

We are more likely to arrive at a sound philosophy of man if we remind ourselves, over and over, that the human being is potentially a very tough creature, though he appears to be ill-fitted for survival. He lacks the teeth and claws of the lion, the speed of the antelope, the warm hair covering of the bear, and much more. He is generically different from other creatures in several ways, one of the most significant of which is that he experiences needs which are truly unique. Men and women can bear hardship, poverty, physical hunger, and pain, but there is one thing which they cannot bear very long, and that is meaninglessness. If they are not provided with meaning in one connection, they will seek it in another. The parable of the impossibility of the permanently empty house is more applicable to our society today than it has ever been in our lives (Matt. 12:43-45).

The more realistic we become about the present, the more hopeful we can be, without wish-thinking, concerning the future, for Christian history, as has been already noted, is replete with examples of inner renewal. Why should this not occur in our particular period of darkness? The paradox, as already suggested, is that realism about our failures is the very seedbed of hope. It is when we admit how far we are from achieving the wholeness which commitment to Christ requires that we can have the courage to make a new start.

The immediate future can, if we do our part, become one of the most exciting periods in the long history of the Christian faith. Part of the hope arises from the reasonable revulsion against the perversions of the faith by which we have recently suffered so greatly. The very recognition of obvious confusion may bring us to our senses and set the stage for genuine advance. Though it is popular to deplore backlash, there are many situations in which it should be welcomed, because it may be of creative value. Revulsion against a fragmented faith may open the door for one which is marked by the vision of wholeness.

A currently revealing example of the value of backlash is occurring in regard to the universities. The general public, as all readers know, is disgusted and rightly disgusted with much that has occurred in recent academic life. One consequence is the sharp increase in the difficulty of raising money for colleges and universities. Hard-working people do not propose to sacrifice in order to keep others in idleness or to encourage destruction. Charles Malik, Professor of Philosophy at the American University in Beirut, and former President of the Assembly of the United Nations, has surprised his listeners by expressing actual gratitude for the academic debacle. His point is that it is a good thing to have revealed, so that all can see, the real weakness of what has been wrongly constituted. He is thinking especially of that kind of education which prides itself upon its abdication of responsibility, so far as moral values are concerned.

An important lesson which we learn from the New Testament is that human failure provided Christians of the first century with one of their most valuable assets, *the recognition of how bad life can be.* The spiritual poverty and immorality of pagan society created a powerful motivation for the new life of the Corinthian Church in which Paul worked and to which he wrote with such eloquence. In a similar fashion, the decay around us now may give "early Christians" of the late twentieth century an adequate reason for renewed dreaming and acting.

If there is one thing clear in our day it is that human beings in our affluent technological age are marked by an apparently insatiable hunger. That there is an urgent desire to be committed, to belong, to enter a committed fellowship, is the deep meaning of much of the shouting and marching and carrying of placards. The more affluent we become, the more insistent the desire appears to be. In one sense, hunger is always good news, and it remains good news even when people seek nourishment with what is obviously stale and unnourishing bread, the intensity of the need being revealed by the poor quality of food to which the hungry person will turn. Even the self-destructive drug-taking tells us primarily, not about the drugs, but about the pathetic hunger of those who desire both meaning and fellowship so desperately that they turn in this deceptive direction in order to try to find them.

The paradox of weakness as the doorway to strength is a truly profound one. John Milton, in his blindness, grasped the paradox more thoroughly than most men have been able to do. In a noble passage in his "Second Defense of the English People" are these words of contemporary significance:

It does not trouble me—though to you it seems painful—to be numbered with the blind, the afflicted, the sorrowful, the weak, since there is hope that I am so much the nearer to the mercy and protection of the Almighty Father. There is a certain way, as the Apostle shows, through weakness to the highest strength. It matters not how weak I may be, so long as in my weakness that immortal and superior strength works more powerfully, so long as in my darkness the light of the divine countenance shines forth more brightly; for then, though feeble, I shall be sublimely strong, sightless and yet endowed with piercing sight. Through this infirmity I can be completed, perfected: in this darkness I can be filled with light. For in truth we blind men are not God's last and slightest care; in proportion as we cannot behold anything except himself, he is disposed to look upon us with the more mercy and kindness.

Intrinsic to an understanding of the Good News is the paradox that a sense of need is fundamentally a blessing. This remains true even when people reach out, in the wrong directions, as they are bound to do sometimes, for their satisfactions. Hunger is not, of course, an unconditional good, since it may lead to false satisfactions, but without it we cannot even make a start in the production of the good life. A sense of need is a necessary condition of spiritual fulfillment, because there is no hope at all for those who do not recognize that they are hungry. Herein lies the radical significance of "Blessed are you that hunger now" (Luke 6:21) and "Blessed are those who hunger and thirst for righteousness" (Matt. 5:6). These are close to the heart of the exciting message which can change human lives.

The major reason for supposing that ours is a time of potential greatness for the faith which has endured in spite of odds, is that today there seems to be a new intensity of spiritual hunger. Christianity won long ago, in another pagan civilization, because it could provide an answer to spiritual emptiness as other systems could not. Our present hope arises from the possibility that the miracle may be reenacted. One of the most encouraging statements of the basis of hope is that of Cardinal Newman when he said of the Church of Christ, "She pauses in her course, and almost suspends her functions; she rises again, and she is herself once more."[6]

6. John Henry Cardinal Newman, *An Essay on the Development of Christian Doctrine* (New York: Longmans, Green & Co., 1949), pp. 415, 416.

II

THE CHURCH
OF THE FUTURE

*God is decreeing to begin some new and great
period in his Church.*

JOHN MILTON

THE CHRISTIAN faith may, indeed, survive in the
future as it has in the past, but does this mean that the
Church will also survive? It is at this point that the questions of so many thoughtful people are becoming insistent.
Is the Church really needed in the new age which we are
entering? Underlying this honest doubt is the more or less
explicit conviction that a churchless Christianity is a practical possibility. Unless we deal seriously with this widespread conviction we are not likely to be able to reach
contemporary minds.

It is not difficult to see why the dream of a churchless
Christianity is currently fashionable. Keep Christ, many
suggest, but set Him free from all of the ecclesiastical
trappings which have accumulated during the years that

have intervened since He lived on earth. Why not return to the simple teachings of the Galilean, eliminating all boards and commissions and fund drives? Isn't there a real danger that the love of Christ may be forgotten in the multitude of conferences, synods, assemblies, and councils? Why not settle for individual love and kindness, without the bother of regular worship, sacraments, and preaching? Because many have noted that the strongest opposition which Christ met on earth was that of the religious establishment, they are bound to wonder whether the same situation does not face Him again today. Perhaps the Church is superfluous, even to Christ Himself.

Part of the doubt about both the efficacy and the necessity of the Church arises from the observed fact that, in numerous areas, congregations are already withering.[1] Consider, for example, the beautiful meetinghouses of New England. It is delightful to any lover of architecture to study the photographs of these wonderful buildings, the white spire in the village being able to lift almost anyone. It is a distinct shock, however, to realize that a good many of these buildings are now used only once a year. Some are not the scenes of gathered fellowships of local residents week after week, and could not even be maintained apart from the efforts of historical societies and local associations formed for the purpose of keeping the physical structures intact. Though we are glad that there are such associations, we are well aware that they are certainly not the Church. However pathetic an unused building may be, regular congregations which include practically no young people are almost equally pathetic. It is actually possible to point to congregations which include nobody under the age of

1. An example of the withering is that the Sunday Schools, once the hope of so many and once truly powerful, are declining in attendance. In one denomination, The United Presbyterian Church, Sunday morning enrollments declined almost a quarter of a million in two years, 1967-1969. See "Why are Church School Enrollments Declining?", *Presbyterian Life*, July 1, 1970, pp. 16, 17.

sixty. Most church buildings, moreover, are far larger than any present need would justify. Is it strange, then, that the idea of a churchless Christianity should be considered as a live option?

That the idea of a churchless Christianity is not intrinsically absurd is evident when we realize that, in most of the world's religions, there has never been anything identical with what we mean by the Church. It is wholly possible to have shrines and priestly orders and scriptures and ceremonies without the existence of gathered communities of ordinary men and women whose faith is nurtured by a living fellowship. Even orders of monks and nuns can exist without the concurrent existence of gathered churches.

Unless we pay close attention to the historical evidence, we are strongly tempted to forget the essential uniqueness of the Christian Church as an expression of the religious life. Indeed, it is a bit shocking to note that the ancient Greeks and Romans who were, in some ways, highly religious, possessed nothing even similar to what we mean by a church. The beautiful temples which we admire, even in ruins, had little or no relation to the kind of experience which we take for granted, with its regularity of group worship, its Sunday School instruction, its suppers, its youth fellowships, it choirs, etc. The leaders of the classic civilization had shrines, priests, and occasional festivals, but all of these together fall short of what we mean by a gathered fellowship of followers of Christ who, though they live and work in the ordinary world, are members one of another.

What we need desperately to understand is that, though it is conceivable that the Christian faith may go on without the organized Church, such an event, if such should occur, would involve a radical alteration in the character of the entire Christian Movement. Because of its realistic estimate of man, Christianity has always seen the necessity of the Church if vitality is to be maintained. Angels might not need the supports and the reminders which the Church provides, but men, as we know very well, are not angels and are not likely to become such. Perhaps the one intellectual giant who understood this best, and was also able to express it most convincingly, was Samuel Johnson. In the midst of his famous essay on Milton he pointed out that any religion "which is animated only by faith and hope, will glide by degrees out of the mind." The human mind, he concluded, needs something in addition to its own unaided resources if it is to be "invigorated and reimpressed." Johnson recognized, in his own interior life, the need of "stated calls to worship, and the salutary influence of example." It seemed to Johnson that the person who claims that he does not need the Church is animated both by arrogance and by ignorance of himself.[2]

The more carefully we study the origins of Christianity, the more we realize that, in the beginning, the Church, far from being something added, was absolutely intrinsic. The New Testament, in fact, is so saturated with the reality of group life that individual religion is the exception rather than the rule. Anyone who repeats, with approbation, the dictum that religion is what a man does with his solitariness can do so only if he is willing to disregard the major Christian witness. On one occasion, it is true, Christ *seemed* to commend individual relgion. This was when He said, "When you pray, go into your room and shut the door and pray to your Father who is in secret" (Matt. 6:6). Though some have drawn from this the odd inference that Christians ought never to engage in group prayer, a careful study of the context fails to substantiate this conclusion. That which Christ was opposing was not prayer in a group, but the prayer of ostentation. He saw the insincer-

2. Samuel Johnson, *Lives of the Poets* (New York: Dolphin Books, Doubleday & Company), Vol. I, pp. 119, 120.

ity of any exhibition in which people claim to be praying when, in actuality, they are seeking to be seen. Christ spoke, in this connection, of those who "love to stand and pray in the synagogues and at the street corners, that they may be seen by men" (Matt. 6:5). That Christ did not, however, teach that all genuine prayer must be carried on in solitude is indicated by His emphasis upon the crucial character of group experience, especially in His affirmation that "where two or three are gathered in my name, there am I in the midst of them" (Matt. 18:20).

We know a great deal more about the meaning of Christianity when we face the fact that Christ engaged in the deliberate effort to form a redemptive fellowship of ordinary men and women. Christ's building of the little fellowship, on which depended the success of His entire enterprise, in both its endurance and its consequent penetration of the world, was the beginning of what we mean by the Church. If the faith is now forced to go on without it, the alteration in character will be so radical that what will remain will be a different reality altogether. What it may be, we naturally cannot know, but we can at least know that it will no longer be the Cause of Christ.

The only reasonable conclusion is that all of the arguments for the probability of the continuance of the faith also turn out to be arguments for the continuance of the *Church*, since the two cannot logically be separated. Individual Christianity is a self-contradiction! Unless there is a sense of "one another" there is no sense of the Living Christ. Though the Church, as we observe it, frequently fills us with frustrations, we know, if we are realists, that it provides the only way in which Christians can be faithful to their Lord. Nothing was accomplished by individual voices crying in the wilderness, but the early fellowship, fallible as it was, produced even the New Testament. It was because of *congregations* that there was a demand for the writing of the Gospels! Furthermore, most of the Epistles have no meaning except in reference to the fellowships to which they are addressed, and even the last book of the Bible begins with letters to seven existing congregations.

The more we ponder, the more we are likely to conclude that the Church will have a future. The Church, of course, may change greatly in its human structure, but the probability is that it will become more important rather than less so. It must become more important because the need for a redemptive fellowship will be increasingly urgent. If men are honest they will recognize the occasional need to be alone, but, if they are also intelligent, they will recognize, at the same time, that what they do alone has far more significance if, at some point in their lives, they experience a deep sharing with other unworthy disciples of the same Lord.

Popular criticism of "organized" Christianity demands careful examination. There can be over-organization, and there can be poor organization, but there is nothing intrinsically wrong about being organized. As a matter of fact, organization is necessary for almost any valuable accomplishment. We are helped, in this regard, if we remember that early Christianity was itself highly organized. Witness the superb system of visitation of which we read in the Pauline Epistles and in the Book of Acts. The way in which the Roman Empire was criss-crossed by the little teams is impressive to any reader who is not so familiar with the story that he takes it for granted. The organization included the collection of funds, in some parts, to help those who suffered in distant places. We are the more amazed at the success of this endeavor when we are reminded of the difficulties of travel and of communication. We cannot avoid the conclusion that, if Christianity had not been "organized," it would not have survived.

The question before thoughtful Christians now is not

whether they will be organized, but *how*. Some inadequate forms and some unproductive fellowships ought clearly to be abandoned. It must never be supposed that there was some perfect form of the Church in the past to which we ought now to return. Indeed, the entire idea of Restoration is one which, the more we analyze it, we are bound to reject as unworthy. Unless we are addicted to primitivism, we see nothing wrong with development. Even Penn's famous phrase "Primitive Christianity Revived," while undoubtedly an effective slogan, was never much more. There is not, in fact, some ideal system of elders and deacons and bishops which once existed and which it is our duty to reproduce. Worship we must experience, but the simple truth is that the entire New Testament does not contain one single order of worship. We can understand a little, from our study of the fourteenth chapter of First Corinthians, of how the early Christians gathered, but we are not furnished with adequate details. Even if we did know how they operated, such knowledge would not provide a norm for our own action today and tomorrow. The Christian faith does not look back to a Golden Age in the past, but always to a more glorious possibility in the future. Whatever the Christians of ancient Corinth did, we should try to improve on their practice, for they were conspicuously imperfect. All of our orientation toward the future is supported by the remarkably hopeful utterance, "I have yet many things to say to you, but you cannot bear them now" (John 16:12).

Why should we assume that there is one perfect way for Christians to be organized? There is surely nothing wrong with variety. The existence of different methods of work and worship is not necessarily something to deplore and may actually produce richness of content. Would it be a gain for the Mennonites, for example, to give up their peculiar witness and thereby become Christians in gen-

eral? It is difficult to defend such a conception with co-
gency. John Milton, in arguing for the advantage to be
gained by variety, employed the metaphor of architecture,
pointing out that the greatest beauty seldom arises from
uniformity. "Neither," he wrote in the *Areopagitica,* "can
every piece of the building be of one form; nay rather, the
perfection consists in this, that out of many moderate var-
ieties and brotherly dissimilitudes that are not vastly dis-
proportional, arises the goodly and graceful symmetry that
commends the whole pile and structure." If the Church of
the future is marked by variety, that will not necessarily be
a false development.

The rebirth of the Church, for which we work and pray,
will not come about by some slight modification of procedure or rearrangement of worship patterns, however desir-
able innovation may sometimes be. The change must be
far more profound. It will not come by the adoption of
increasingly bizarre architecture, for that is obviously superficial. Indeed, there are indications that the era of con-
centration upon the erection of physical structures of any
kind is already over.

The profound change, which goes to the heart of the
matter, is centered on the revolutionary idea of the *ministry.* Worship we have long had, and worship we must
continue to have, but worship is by no means sufficient; in
truth, it is not nearly so important as is ministry. Some
Christians are surprised when their attention is called to
the relative emphasis of the New Testament regarding
worship and ministry. Though worship is mentioned only
infrequently, ministry is the constant theme. The characteristic call is not a call to attend public worship, but to
minister to one another. At the heart of the Gospel is the
revolutionary injunction, "Whoever would be great
among you must be your servant" (Matt. 20:26). We must
never forget that servant and minister are exact synonyms.

Christians cannot survive in the future without gathered fellowships, but we need to examine more rigorously the central purpose of the repeated gatherings. We are called to gather, not primarily to attend a "meeting for worship," but, far more, to share in a "meeting for preparation for the ministry in common life."

Few items of the gospel are more moving than the brief sentence, "Something greater than the temple is here" (Matt. 12:6). Much of our endeavor, as we face the future of the Church, is that of trying to understand together what the character of this "something greater" may be. We get some hint of what the "something greater" may have been, in Christ's own dream, when we note where He placed the emphasis. The Church, as He envisioned it, was made up of those who were engaged in a healing task. Because people were harassed and helpless, like sheep without a shepherd, workers were needed, *and these workers were the Church!*

It is a great moment in any life when a Christian comes to realize that the Church, as Christ formed it long ago, was not a crowd watching a performance, but persons engaged in a ministry to other persons. We cannot appreciate all that Christ had in mind when he spoke of the Church, but we have made at least one step in that direction when we see that He was recruiting a society of ministers in daily life. If this vision can be implemented, the future of the Church is no longer doubtful! The conception of Christ as the perpetual Recruiter, and the members of the Church as His team, is one of such intrinsic appeal that it is not dependent upon changing fashions, including fashions of theology. The Church is the enlargement of the "Twelve," and, like the original Twelve, it is bound to include unworthy persons. Part of the miracle is the demonstrated fact that unworthy persons, when ignited by the central fire of Christ, are able to ignite other unworthy persons. After leaving the synagogue at Nazareth, to which He may never have returned, Christ started something really new in religion. The key sentence, which shows the expulsive character of the new fellowship, is as follows: "And he called to him the twelve, and began to send them out" (Mark 6:7). Here was something conspicuously greater than the temple and its ritual. Whereas the temple had been centripetal, the Church was intended to be centrifugal.

Once we are able to understand that emphasis upon the ministry is the key to new vitality, our strategy becomes clear. What we need to do is to draw into the ministry the various groups which, for one reason or another, are now partly excluded from it. The exciting adventure centers largely upon the effort to liberate the potential human forces which are now largely untapped. It is in the employment of wasted powers that there can be the greatest single difference between the Church of today and the Church of tomorrow. The involvement of those who are not now members of Christ's team may produce important changes both in their lives and in the life of the world. We are driven to this when we realize how poor we are and how rich we might be.

Four groups, potentially valuable to the Christian Cause, are, at the present time, relatively untapped human resources. These four are *laymen, women, retired persons,* and *youth.* Some persons in each of these four groups are now involved in the promotion of the Christian Cause, but they represent only a tiny fraction of the power which is currently available. It will require more thinking than we have yet employed to know how to liberate these urgently needed but partially undeveloped human assets. Because failure to make use of what is available is not only sinful, but stupid, we must give careful thought to this fourfold task.

1. *The inclusion of laymen in the ministry* has already been partly accomplished, though much remains to be done. Indeed, the theory and practice of the lay ministry has been the greatest single mark of emerging vitality in the Church of the twentieth century. The crucial date in this emergence, so far as our century is concerned, is 1931. In that year of deep economic depression John R. Mott gave the Ayer Lectures at the Colgate-Rochester Divinity School and started a fundamentally new chapter in the life of the Church. The title of the lectures, and also of the book which was published in 1932, was *Liberating the Lay Forces of Christianity.* Dr. Mott was not, of course, the first to encourage lay religion, but he was able to catch the imagination of Christian people as few before him had done. As Chairman of the International Missionary Council and President of the World Alliance of Young Men's Christian Associations, his words carried great weight, especially among contemporary students.

Much has occurred during the subsequent forty years, in the growth of the lay ministry, and numerous voices have been added to Dr. Mott's, but in many ways his appeal was original. What was unique was the concept of liberation. He saw men of wisdom and experience who were largely unused because they were bound by a false idea, the idea that the Christian ministry is the proprietary domain of clergymen. The very notion that there is a genuine difference between clergy and laity must be recognized as a heresy, the division between them being the most deadly of all schisms! Partly because of the pioneering thinking of Dr. Mott, the conviction that in Christ there is neither lay nor clerical has become one of the most liberating ideas of the twentieth century. Not all accept or understand this bold conception, even yet, but a good many, including some readers of this book, realize that only by faithfulness to it can we erect something bigger than the temple.

It would be foolish to fail to admit that there is resistance to lay liberation and that there are numerous congregations in which no serious start has been made in this redemptive innovation. There are, indeed, supposedly committed Christians who see nothing intrinsically absurd about the expectation that one man should be inspired to speak fifty-two times a year, while the others are never expected to have the experience at all. The easy procedure is to go on with a society in which a few speak and many listen, but this is the road to death.

It must be frankly admitted that some members actually prefer the position of noninvolvement. Obviously it is much less demanding to settle for attendance at some gatherings, combined with a modest financial support, than to enter into the ministry. There is nothing really surprising about the fact that so many prefer to delegate their religious responsibility to an individual who is hired to do the task, much as they hire a man to make out income tax returns. People often prefer this because it is less costly, but in religion the results of such a division of labor are uniformly damaging. Christianity, in spite of its miraculous history, decays unless a fair proportion of its adherents accept joyously the conception of the Church of Christ as a servant society, made up of those who are engaged in the work of the world at the same time that they are engaged in being Christ's representatives. Some teachers have been saying this for a generation, and there have been visible effects of this teaching, but more must now pursue the theme, because the idea has not taken sufficient hold.

Elevation of the potential ministry of the lay Christian involves no depreciation of the work of the pastor. Indeed, emphasis upon lay ministry, far from making the pastor less important, makes him far more so. "I do not," said Mott in 1931, "share the view that the Christian ministry does not have so important and so necessary a function as in the past."[3] The reason why the idea of the Church, as a society of ministers in common life, requires the pastoral ministry is that the pastor is the one person who is most likely to be able, if he gives his attention to the task, "to build up, to train, to inspire, and to direct the lay forces." There is a place for the ministry of persons who are employed full time in factories and shops and government offices, but there is, without contradiction, a place for the ministry of men who are freed from the necessity of secular earning. Someone needs to work at the job of *calling out the latent forces.*

The Church of the future will have pastors for the simple reason that vital lay religion does not emerge unless somebody works at the task of its development. The primary professional ministry of the future will undoubtedly be the ministry of encouragement. What is more exciting than the release of human powers which have long lain dormant? We need genuine professionals, not in the sense that they are skilled in ceremonial performances, but in the far deeper sense that they have learned the skill of drawing out the powers of other men. This is precisely what is meant today by the "equipping" or the "enabling" ministry (Eph. 4:12), and it ought to become the center of professional pastoral training in the future. In the Church of the future the liberator of other men's powers will be more, rather than less, important. We may not actually employ the term "liberator" rather than "pastor," but that is what we shall have to mean if there is to be a new chapter in the life of the Church.

It is important to do some new thinking about religious

3. John R. Mott, *Liberating the Lay Forces of Christianity* (New York: The Macmillan Company, 1932), p. 93.

professionalism. This is required as we reexamine our total enterprise, in the willingness to omit anything which does not meet the real needs of men. We soon realize that there is a sense in which religious professionalism is undesirable, and also a sense in which it is necessary. Professionalism is deeply wrong if it inhibits the involvement of the non-professionals. This is often what results when a congregation employs a staff which is too large. There is, of course, the consequent problem of raising money to pay salaries, rather than to feed the hungry, but this is not the primary difficulty. Far worse is the almost inevitable undermining of the unpaid involvement of the ordinary members of what is supposed to be a team. Over and over, when the question is asked why lay members are not active participants in the conduct of public worship, as regular readers of the Scriptures, the standard answer is that associate pastors have been employed and that they have to be used visibly. Whenever staff members perform duties which lay members need to do, this is a sign of sickness rather than of health.

The emphasis upon the liberation of laymen must never make the mistake of denying that there is a significant place for the professional. There is nothing wrong with being a professional writer, with the conscious development of clarity; there is, likewise, nothing wrong with being a professional speaker, using all of the powers of speech to convey the truth and knowing when to stop, as the amateur often does not. We need men who are genuine professionals in listening to others, drawing out of them ideas and hopes, of which they might not have become aware, without intelligent assistance.

2. *Women constitute a second group of Christians whose liberation would add enormously to the power of Christ in the world.* Though, in comparison with other world religions, the Christian record in the involvement of women is rela-

tively good, it is not good enough. Women were Christ's intimate companions (Luke 8:2); women stood at the cross; women reported the resurrection; and women are mentioned frequently in the New Testament Epistles. In the noble passage in which the term "Yokefellow" appears as a synonym for a practicing Christian recruit, there is reference to two women who, says Paul, "labored side by side with me in the gospel" (Phil. 4:3). Though Paul, at one time in his career, took a dim view of speaking on the part of women (I Cor. 14:34, 35), he advanced, as he reached the climax of his religious experience, to the height of recognizing that sexual distinctions are absolutely meaningless in the service of Christ. This is the clear significance of Galatians 3:28. Because we are "all one in Christ Jesus," it follows logically, Paul saw, that "there is neither male nor female."

In spite of this brave start, women have not been used in the Church exactly as men. In numerous contemporary congregations the women worshipers outnumber the men, sometimes by as much as two to one, but most of the important leadership is still in male hands. We do not need to subscribe to the rhetoric of the Women's Liberation Movement to see that this situation is deeply wrong, and it is especially clear that it is stupid, when the Church is literally fighting, against great odds, for its very life. It is foolish to neglect available power when it is desperately needed. Just as, forty years ago, John R. Mott started us thinking seriously about "liberating the lay forces of Christianity," so now, in our effort to create an intelligent future, we must help one another to think carefully about liberating the female forces. This is how the Christian movement proceeds; one wave of liberation follows another! We must try to see which sector needs major attention at each particular time.

Women are, of course, used in the contemporary

Church, but they are not, for the most part, used in the ways where their contribution would add the greatest strength. Women cook congregational suppers; women teach children and other women; women organize missionary societies; women operate social circles; women serve on altar guilds. Having made such a list, we soon realize that we are hard pressed if we try to enlarge it. Where we fail is in the encouragement of Christian women to provide intellectual leadership. That such leadership is possible is proven by reference to the work of Dorothy Sayers, Olive Wyon, Georgia Harkness, and a few more, but it is not possible to extend such a list as we might wish to do.

The possible employment of women's intellectual life provides more concrete hope than can be found almost anywhere. In spite of the increasing fashion of employment of women outside the home, in business and industry, it is still true that women, on the whole, have more free time in their lives than do most men. After the children have departed, there is often a magnificent chance to start a new productive chapter, if only women could have the imagination to see the opportunity. Why are we not intelligent enough to see that the ministry of women is our unexploited asset? There is no doubt about the dedication of women, often surpassing that of men; the doubt is whether we can harness the dedication in more than trivial ways. Most men, however devoted they may be, are too tired at the end of competitive days of labor to engage in creative thinking, but there are thousands of women who do not encounter this handicap to rational inquiry.

We need help at almost every point in the articulation of our faith. This articulation cannot be accomplished except as there emerges an entire generation of Christian intellectuals. These are more likely to come among women than from any other source, but they will not appear unless we produce a mood of expectancy. Women may surpass men in the modern world in setting up book tables to help the members and attenders in the guidance of their reading; women may start serious classes in theology to help distraught and confused people to think clearly about the deepest issues of their lives; women may produce books which will do for their generation what Dorothy Sayers did so magnificently for hers.

Most people, when they speak of the ministry of women, think at once of women clergy, a conception which some reject. Though we have women preachers, and though Lutherans have now decided, for the first time in their history, to ordain women, the number is small. For example, although women comprise 57.4 percent of the membership of the United Presbyterian Church, they comprise only one half of one percent of the teaching elders and only 15.75 percent of the ruling elders. These figures will undoubtedly change radically in the immediate future, because there is no good reason why women should not speak and counsel precisely as men do, but this is not where the main growth seems to be coming. The main growth is that of the emergence of new ministries which women themselves are able to invent and encourage. One indication of what is expected is the appearance in 1970 of a new book by a Christian woman, who started writing at the Southern Baptist Convention at New Orleans in June, 1969.[4]

Some women, even more than men, may resist the idea of a Christian intellectual vocation for themselves, because they are so keenly aware of their inadequacy. The clear answer to this objection is that people can *grow* and that they are supposed to grow. One woman at The Church of the Saviour in Washington, D.C. was practically illiterate

4. Martha Nelson, *The Christian Woman in the Working World* (Nashville: The Broadman Press).

when she was enrolled in Christian study, but before her death she was a resource leader for the pastor, Gordon Cosby, in regard to some details of modern theology. Furthermore, we are helped by remembering the way in which inferior powers may be glorified by proper use. That most of the early Christians felt inadequate is indicated by Paul's specific words. "Few of you," he wrote, "are men of wisdom, by any human standard" (I Cor. 1:26, NEB). One in our century who understood this thoroughly and stated it clearly was John D. Rockefeller, Jr. Speaking in 1916, he said, "In carrying on the world's work, the Lord is not able to select perfect tools that are exactly fitted for each requirement; He has to use such human instruments as are available."[5]

3. *The third major human resource that is essentially unexploited is that of retired people.* Now that it is standard for those who work both with hand and brain to retire at the age of sixty-five or sooner, we are producing a vast human reservoir waiting to be tapped. We have, of course, given some attention to this phenomenon, especially in the creation of retirement communities, but, for the most part, we have not seen the possibilities so far as the Christian Movement is concerned. Because of better public health, many retired people are physically and mentally strong, with an accumulation of wisdom about life which comes from long experience. It is fundamentally ridiculous to assume that such people should concentrate on playing shuffleboard for twenty years! But what is the alternative?

The most beneficent change in regard to retired people is a change in their own self-image, and this is the point at which the Christian faith can make a genuine contribution. *For the Christian, retirement means liberation for service, and*

5. John D. Rockefeller, Jr., *Proceedings of the Thirty-ninth International Convention of Young Men's Christian Associations of North America* (New York: Association Press, 1916), p. 501.

it means nothing else. The retired Christian physician, if he understands the gospel, asks where people need medical care, but cannot afford it. Liberation from the necessity of earning, which retirement income accomplishes more and more, simply places numerous modest persons in the same category to which John R. Mott belonged all of his mature life. Very early he was "liberated" by a group of men who undertook to pay his bills so that he could give himself to a career of unmercenary service. Because this is an idea which is little understood, and often not even contemplated, it is one in which, by its dissemination, the Church of tomorrow can make a difference. It must be made clear, however, that the opportunity of the retired Christian is not to serve the Church, but the *world.*

4. *Young People constitute not only the greatest challenge to the Church of the future, but also its greatest hope.* The evidence of the probable continuance of the Church in succeeding centuries is valid, but its validity depends on the possibility of attracting a far larger proportion of young people. There is good reason to believe that this can be done, but it will not be done unless we meet the conditions. One of the conditions is an honest admission of how radically we are failing in gaining the participation of youth at the present time. There is, as anyone can see, a vast reservoir of moral idealism, a fervent eagerness to participate in liberating causes, and an almost unlimited willingness to engage in sacrifice if the cause justifies it, but, in the eyes of the majority of young people, these features of contemporary living have no connection with the Church of Jesus Christ. There are, of course, youth programs in most congregations, and many of these are generously financed, but there is little doubt that most of them are failing to do what needs to be done. The modern Church involves the very young, as it involves a fair proportion of the mature, but the failure in regard to those

between these is almost total. This is what must change!

When the failure is so great, it is reasonable to look for some really serious mistake. We soon realize that such a mistake, if it exists, is probably entailed in our philosophy rather than in our methods. Actually, our methods are reasonably good. We provide excellent quarters; we establish coffee houses; we organize camps; we employ counselors. Necessary as these may be, they are grossly insufficient if we start with the wrong major premise. We begin to see how wrong our basic approach may be when we realize that most of our youth programs are set up to *serve youth.* The young people, of course, sense this at once. They know that others are paying for their refreshments and their entertainment. But the tragedy is that entertainment is precisely what they do not need, because it is what they already have in superabundance.

What young people need is *to be needed,* and to *know* that they are needed. If they could be convinced that the world is plagued with a sense of meaninglessness, and that they can have an answer to confusion and perplexity, their relationship to the Church might be altered radically. In short, the only way to attract youth is to draw them into a ministry! They are now trying, in great numbers, to minister to physical hunger or to overcome racial discrimination, but few have been helped to see that the deepest problems of men and women are spiritual. They have not been told that the human harvest is being spoiled for lack of workers, and that they can be the workers. They have not been told of the toil in which they must engage in order to prepare their minds so that they can be effective in reaching others, and particularly those of their own age, who are harassed and helpless.

The Christian faith does not need to go outside itself in order to find a principle which can produce a radical change in the attraction of young people. The principle which is effective, when seriously applied, is inherent in the moral revolution which Christ came to inaugurate. There is no way to exaggerate either the theoretical or practical importance of the words, "The Son of man also came not to be served but to serve" (Mark 10:45). Modern youth will not be enrolled in the Christian Cause until they are recruited as members of the servant team, ministering to the varied needs of God's children. The motivation for this service is greater within the pattern of the Church than within that of any social agency, because Christ speaks to inner as well as to outer needs. Preparation for this kind of ministry is necessarily difficult and long, but that only makes it more appealing to the best of our young people.

Though great numbers of young people are wholly outside the life of the Church at this moment, this can change rapidly, as it has changed before. In many areas the moral debacle is so great that a shift of the pendulum is almost inevitable. The obvious weakness of a permissive morality, which is ultimately self-destructive, may lead to a new Puritanism. If it is a Puritanism like that of John Milton who "was made for whatever is arduous," that will constitute an advance of genuine magnitude. Already there are signs that this is beginning to occur, and frequently the young people are more advanced on this road than are their teachers. Some who have discovered at first hand the fact that the pseudo-gods, such as drugs and promiscuity, are fundamentally delusive, are turning, with open eyes, to the Living God.

III

THE NEW
STRATEGIES

The ages of faith are the ages of rationalism.
ALFRED NORTH WHITEHEAD

IT WAS indicative of the genius of Archbishop William Temple that he saw the Church militant as a society which was only half complete. There is a tremendous appeal in any structure which is only partly finished and which cries out, consequently, for completion. The Church of Christ is such a structure. It possesses a sure foundation, but the superstructure that can be erected upon it may be far greater than anything we have ever known in practice. As it is the pathetic sight of half-men which encourages us in the pursuit of wholeness, so it is the unsatisfactory character of the Church as we know it that spurs us to the work of completion. It is equally disloyal to be satisfied with the Church as it is, and to abandon it as a lost cause.

As we engage today in the holy yet profoundly humbling task of helping to create the future, it is necessary to have a clear understanding of where the weakness of the contemporary Christian Movement is, and also of where the existing power resides. Fortunately, it takes no great genius to see both of these. The most obvious contemporary weakness concerns what has historically been known as the *parish*. The parish pattern which was effective for a long time, though it is seldom effective now, is that of people living in a single area which is served by a single church organization with its building or buildings. Regardless of denominational labels, each such unit was really a Community Church. It is this particular pattern which is outmoded. There are many reasons for the obsolescence of the parish conception, one important cause being that of modern mobility. A new church is established west of the river, ostensibly to serve the people of the particular area, but soon, if there is any vitality at all, the people who are involved are almost as likely to live east of the river as west of it. When people get into cars, it is as easy to drive four miles as one mile.

The parish was a natural conception in agricultural America, and even in our early industrial culture, but today, almost everywhere, the basis for it is gone. There are, of course, strong existing congregations, but they are seldom limited by geography. It is not primarily by proximity, but by a unity of convictions, loyalties, and hopes that people are drawn together redemptively. There may or may not be a new basis of unity among people, but it is certain that the dominant factor will not be geographical.

The decline of the Community Church idea is matched by the decline of the prestige congregation. In the long past, and even in the recent past, it has been well understood where people should belong if they desire to get ahead socially. The prestige congregation has normally worshiped in a splendid building with an impressive location, sometimes on a hill. Also there has been eloquent preaching and music which meets professional standards of excellence. Consequently, attenders were long assured of a performance which was not embarrassing. Furthermore, one was likely to meet the right people.

Now the decay of the prestige fellowship is almost universal. The congregations suffering most are those whose ushers wear striped pants. The slick performance, with the paid choir, the popular preacher, and the professional soprano soloist, is almost nonexistent, though vestiges appear in a few areas. The paradox is that what has been proudly named "First Church" has empty pews more often than not, while structures erected by offbeat sects tend to be crowded. It is what we call "Main Line Churches" which are suffering most seriously. A congregation with a single uneducated pastor often reaches more people, and has a far higher level of proportionate giving, than does a supposedly affluent congregation with a large staff of trained leaders.

There are many reasons for this observed paradox, most of them having to do with the essential nature of Christ's Church. The very idea of "First Church," with scarcely concealed pride whenever the words are employed, is, as we ought to have known, a contradiction in terms, for it aspires precisely to what Christ rejected (Mark 10:43, 44). The notion that there is some fundamental preeminence by virtue of being the first to organize in a community is one which is curious when it comes from a Christian. There is, by contrast, a congregation in Ceylon which employs the inspired name, "The Church of the Servant Lord." What is surprising is that such nomenclature has not been more widely copied.

Some of the decline of the Main Line congregation

arises from the fact that it has served to accentuate the temptation to detachment. Even when the building is ecclesiastically correct, with divided chancel and nave, and with dignified pews rather than theater chairs, the "balcony mentality" is subtly encouraged. After all, listening to the trained choir is not radically different from listening in the Academies of Music. The pastor has been expected to put on a good performance, with a well-prepared address, and, if he performs well, he is rewarded at the front door by fulsome praise. All of this, of course, can be a pleasant experience, but it is radically different from personal involvement in the work of a missionary team.

The Main Line Church is not hopeless; the dead bones can be made to live; but new life will come only by a radical alteration in pattern. The nature of the required alteration is suggested, in part, by observing where it is that the real power resides today, so far as the Christian Cause is concerned. The power is often demonstrated in what, with some condescension, we call the *sects.* These are groups of Christians who have little social standing, who gather in modest structures, and whose leaders are hardly recognized as clergymen, but who take their faith with such seriousness that they give sacrificially of both time and money. The important thing to know is that such groups are growing rapidly at the same time that prestigious congregations are either dwindling or failing to keep up with the rate of population growth. In this regard the sects are in sharp contrast, not only to dominant Protestantism, but even to Roman Catholicism which now faces serious retrenchment.

The contrasting conceptions of Church and sect, long recognized, were clarified for many literate Christians by Ernst Troeltsch in a famous book published in Germany in 1911 under the title *Die Soziallehren der christlichen Kirc-*

hen und Gruppen. [1] This book was translated into excellent English by Olive Wyon in 1931. Troeltsch has taught an entire generation of Christian scholars to see that Church and sect have long existed side by side, both being important for the entire Christian Cause. Though the two patterns are sometimes combined, the general lines of demarcation are clear. The church-type of Christian organization is normally associated with centers of secular power and may even be part of the legal establishment. The Church of England is an obvious and familiar example of the church-type, because it makes no rigorous demands upon its members, and because it claims no separation from the world. Such a religious organization is always marked by "an all-inclusive, non-ethical basis of Church membership." [2]

The sect exists in contrast to the established or semiestablished Church in almost every feature of its life and work, the lives of the members being marked by practices which distinguish them sharply from the patterns of the world around them. A conspicuous example of this is that provided by the Seventh Day Adventists, whose rhythm of the week differs from that of most of their neighbors. The members of a sect usually have less money, less formal education, and less access to the centers of political influence than have the members of the church-type organization. Thus sect membership is costly in almost every way. We need to understand why, in spite of this, the sect-type of Christian society is conspicuously more able to exhibit spiritual power than is its major alternative.

The power of the sect obviously derives from the fact that it provides needy men and women with the experience of a committed fellowship. This more than counter-

---

1. *The Social Teaching of the Christian Churches,* two vols. (New York: Harper Torchbooks, 1960).
2. Ibid., Vol. II, p. 695.

balances the general lack of learning. Whatever else they are, the sect members are not primarily spectators, since all know that they are sorely needed. In some instances, as among Jehovah's Witnesses, all look upon themselves as both ministers and missionaries, often going from door to door. This is done deliberately at those times on Sundays when other groups are supposedly engaged in public worship. This increases the vulnerability of those who are found in their own homes at such an hour, the ordinary excuses being rendered unconvincing. At the same time the lack of fine buildings counters the tendency to glorify a shrine. The sect has concentrated upon the creation of a believing, witnessing fellowship and on nothing else. That it provides great numbers of perplexed people with what they think they need is beyond doubt.

Firsthand experience of life in an unfashionable but deeply committed Christian group is truly revealing to one whose chief contact has been with the more respectable variety. The author recently shared with such a group an all-day retreat, in which most of the adult members shared continuously. Such an experience is almost unthinkable in the standard church, with a multitude of other responsibilities, many of which take priority of those connected with the gospel. The members of the unfashionable group, whose very existence was unknown to most of their neighbors, met to consider the character of their faith, their ministry, their reading, and their outreach. The donation of time was in marked contrast to the habit of those who suppose that one hour a week is a generous offering. In nearly every detail, the contrast between sect and Church was favorable to the sect. As the retreat developed, it became increasingly clear that the participants really knew one another and also that they accepted an essentially unlimited liability for one another's welfare. Such personal involvement is rare in the fashionable congregation, whose "churchgoers" would not even recognize many of their fellow attenders if they were to meet them on the street.

In all honesty we must understand that the sect has its own dangers. Perhaps the greatest danger is that of the spiritual pride which is an overreaction to subtle persecution on the part of both the world and established Christianity. At its worst the sect mentality produces a marked Pharisaism based upon the consciousness of good works. This is increased, as Troeltsch observed, by the obligation which the sect member feels, "to consider the Church as degenerate."[3] The consequent sense of superiority arises from the relative lack of involvement in the complex and frustrating problems of general culture, including those of science and philosophy. But when we have seen this, it also behooves us to see that the strength of the sect tends to overbalance its weaknesses. What is despised becomes "the head of the corner" (Ps. 118:22). There has been a widespread and unargued assumption that the familiar movement from sect to Church has been a sign of advance, but it is time to question this assumption. We have often been wrong in our judgment on this score, and the evidence that we have been wrong lies in the comparative fruits.

More and more it is from the hitherto despised Christian groups that genuine intellectual vigor emerges. We suppose, in our unchallenged snobbery, that it is the products of First Church who make the high marks in academic life, but there is now evidence to challenge this comforting assumption. Among those who rise to the top in learned accomplishments, a surprising number are children of small shop owners or factory foremen who, more often than not, have drawn their spiritual nourishment from unfashionable Christian groups. It is safer to bet, academ-

3. Ibid., Vol. I, p. 337.

ically, on the children of the hard hats than on the children of the country-club crowd. When we study the affiliations of the ablest graduate students we begin to comprehend this really surprising fact. This result is part of the whole problem of affluence with which the establishment is afflicted. We are told specifically that it is "the delight in riches" which, along with "the cares of the world," chokes the word so that "it proves unfruitful" (Matt. 13:22).

If we are wise we shall expect future leaders in all kinds of secular pursuits to emerge from groups which are normally despised. Professor Timothy Smith, of Johns Hopkins University, himself a Nazarene, has made a special study of academic eminence arising in unexpected places. Leadership may actually emerge from Pentecostal and other fringe groups, in which hard work and the Puritan ethic have not yet been undermined by ridicule. The unfashionable sect is almost the only unit of Christendom which is able to generate the kind of disciplined commitment which can equal that of the Communist Movement. The sect, then, may not be the complete answer to vitality in the future, since it involves defects of its own making, but it offers some elements which any enduring Christian order must demonstrate. What the future of the sect may be no man can know, but we can at least recognize its present vitality.

There is hope, not for faith in general, but for certain specific kinds. The kinds which provide the strongest basis for encouragement are those in which there is real belief, in which the lay resources are liberated because involved, and in which a balance is maintained between inner piety and outer service. A promising hypothesis is that this fruitful combination may be found, neither in the Church-type alone, nor in the sect-type alone, but in some creative combination of the two.

We get some idea of what the creative combination may

be when we study the many kinds of small Christian groups which have already emerged in this century. Our century has not been marked primarily by the appearance of new denominations; on the contrary, it has witnessed some decrease in denominations because of mergers. The novel groups bear more similarity to an order than to a denomination, because they usually cut across established lines. That the participants in the new orders are known by various names is not important because they have more in common than in difference. The new labels with which we have become familiar are Faith at Work, Yokefellows, International Christian Leadership, The Twelve, The Diciplined Order of Christ, Koinonia, Laos, etc. On the whole these are not groupings which are in any sense anti-Church, since they are, in every case, consciously devoted to the revitalization of the Church of Christ. The "small group movement" and the "Church renewal movement" have combined in practice. This is undoubtedly a sign of hope.

Though the new units which have emerged are not trying to supersede or bypass the Church, they produce encouragement in that they provide something which, in the conventional church, has long been lacking. Because many ordinary Christian units have failed to stress (1) common commitment, (2) a shared ministry, (3) a voluntary discipline, and (4) a genuine fellowship, it is not surprising that movements have arisen to meet these four important requirements.

Perhaps the most significant advance in Christian experience in our generation has been in the understanding of what the character of the ideal Christian unit really is. For too long we assumed uncritically that there was something intrinsically valuable about a gathering based on geographical proximity. All the farmers and their families had so much in common that the church gathering was, indeed, the right one for them. But this may not be true under changing circumstances. Always there must be the gathered fellowship, if power is to be generated, but the gathered fellowship may be expressed in units markedly different from those deemed normal only a generation ago. Why should they not be based upon vocation, as in a Guild of Christian Doctors, or upon personal need, as in Alcoholics Anonymous, or upon manner of life, as among prisoners?

We have begun to learn a great deal from prisoners, particularly those who wear Christ's Yoke behind prison walls. These people can sometimes grasp what the supposedly free citizens are likely to miss. For example, here is an excerpt from a letter written by an inmate at the Lewisburg Federal Prison:

> I have been going through some severe struggles with myself concerning Christ, myself and the Church. I only wish I could report some answers, but the struggle goes on. . . . I still have not solidified my position. People keep saying "work within the Church to help make it better," but this is not an idea that I can accept—blindly—without many questions which still need answers.
>
> I still believe, and always will, that one of the greatest things to happen to Christianity in this century has been the founding of Yokefellows. But here is where one of my questions is situated. One of the seven disciplines is to worship in a church. My Yokefellow group is what I feel Christ would approve of as a church. It provides worship, fellowship and thought; I do not find these in church, either here or in the churches outside. I keep asking myself if I believe Christ would support the denominational churches that we have today. And I keep getting the same answer—No.

Any sincere Christian is bound to be a bit shaken by this prisoner's thinking and writing. He really makes us wonder if outsiders are being cheated. Numerous prisoners have lost their faith in established congregations, including that of the prison chapel, not because they desire something less, but because they demand something more. How curious that some men find, behind prison walls, a reality which they have never found in Christian societies outside! One prisoner writes with words impossible to dismiss: "I can only say with all sincerity, that were it necessary for me to have been in prison in order to have come to know Christ, I would not have missed it for all the world."

As careful readers of the work of Troeltsch may remember, the German scholar predicted the emergence of new forms of association "equally remote from both Church and sect."[4] This is occurring and will, judging by present indications, occur increasingly in the future, though the particular forms of association are different from anything Troeltsch or his contemporaries imagined. We have had the church-type and the sect-type associations for centuries, and we have long had separate "orders" within the Church, but now we seem to be developing something radically new. The hope is that the new voluntary associations, being orders of a new character in the world, rather than separated from it, may demonstrate reality in membership, without the exclusiveness and the self-righteousness of the sect.

One of the most hopeful developments is the *Cadre.* This term is beginning to appear as a designation for a small group of committed Christians intent on making a difference in the world. Though the actual structure may be similar to what we have known for a generation in groups dedicated to prayer, sharing, study, witness, and service, the deliberate use of military terminology is helpful to some in the sharpening of the focus. The people who

4. Ibid., Vol. I, p. 381.

employ this term do so partly because they are aware of military language in the New Testament and that such language has often been used by peaceful Christians. On balance, however, it may be better to avoid the military term and adopt, instead, one with an excellent history, i.e., *the band.* If this is reminiscent of the members of Gideon's Band (Judg. 7:2 ff.), of their modern namesakes who have worked a modern miracle in the distribution of the Scriptures, and of the Student Volunteer Band, that is all to the good. The term is valuable in that it suggests a vivid contrast to the mild religion with which we have, for too long, been afflicted.

The modern band is a definite group of human membership, which may include women as well as men and is normally limited to about fifteen persons. The group follows a discipline which, though it is accepted voluntarily, is not regarded lightly. The members realize that discipline is one of the chief marks of a soldier, and they seek to be good soldiers of Jesus Christ (II Tim. 2:3). Far from having their discipline imposed from without, the members construct their own interior guide lines, *together.* Usually the discipline includes both the inner life and the outer service. The group cannot survive unless the members are tough with themselves, giving temporal priority to their times of meeting, to private devotions, and to acts of human compassion. For the most part the compassionate service, it is found, need not be that of some new project which the group inaugurates and conducts as a team, but rather an invigoration of the service which each member is encouraged to render in connection with his own regular way of life. For example, the insurance agent, who belongs, may be helped by the others in this group to see new possibilities of ministry as he deals daily with his clients.

The signal advantage of the new kind of fellowship appears in the lives of people who, though they have tried to be loyal members of established congregations, have been less than thrilled. They attend church on Sunday morning, but come away feeling that they have not accomplished anything. The mood of discouragement deepens as they become convinced that they have not done anything except to occupy space in a pew and add one unit to the statistical report. The thoughtful person naturally asks, "What has been accomplished?" Each may, indeed, add his little candlelight to the other candlelights, but is that all that ought to be expected of me as a member of Christ's team? In a deep sense, the search for a better way is the result of "the revolution of rising expectations."

What the individual who joins the group experiences, is often truly novel to him. Suddenly, he has moved from the bleachers to the gridiron. One, in a reporting letter, makes the following surprised observation: "Small groups can do more than large groups because there is no room for freeloaders." Important as this observation is, we must never suppose that mere smallness is a sufficient condition for the emergence of vitality. It is the combination of size, purpose, and discipline which works wonders. The group which comes together merely for sociability is likely to lose, before long, even the sociability, whereas the mutual affection is a by-product of the participation in a common aim. Profound fellowship is always *directional* in origin; it comes from looking together in the same direction. Nearly all the best things of life are by-products.

Sometimes the small group becomes a genuine healing agency. Able psychiatrists may also be committed Christians, and among these are a few who have discovered that the primary unit for recovery of mental health need not be the meeting of the individual with his physician, but may be the caring group. One psychiatrist who has been particularly successful in this "transaction" is Thomas A. Harris, of Sacramento.[5]

An increasing number of small groups, not only in America, but also in other parts of the world, now find strength in calling themselves Yokefellows. Indeed, the rediscovery of this term, first by Dwight L. Moody in the nineteenth century, and more recently by various persons in the twentieth century, has been truly revolutionary. Suddenly, by employing the Biblical term, we discover a word which denotes a person who is a minister, but not a clergyman. Yokefellows, being those who labor side by side in the gospel (Phil. 4:3), are the exact opposite of spectators! The reason why they are yoked together is that, first of all, they are yoked with Christ, wearing His Yoke with Him (Matt. 11:29). Consequently, all are in the ministry, whatever their secular occupations may be; all accept voluntary discipline as an alternative to empty freedom; all find or make a genuine fellowship in which, with unlimited liability and vulnerability, they strengthen one another. They do not join an organization in the ordinary fashion, for there is no official roster of such groups. They encourage others, by whatever name, to copy and use that which they may be able to produce. The new order, which is constantly growing, seeks, like Alcoholics Anonymous, to be *nonpossessive,* like the Church, to be *inclusive,* and, like the sect, to be *demanding.* The new order, which stands in contrast, not only to the church-type society, but also to the sect-type society, includes both women and men, both clergymen and laymen, both scholars and those with modest education. That there are no distinctions of either race or denomination is so obvious that it is seldom mentioned.

5. See the book by Dr. Harris, *I'm OK—You're OK* (New York: Harper & Row, 1969).

The dream which is unfolding is especially important at this time because it provides seekers with a genuine alternative to two kinds of loneliness, the loneliness of the solitary individual, and the loneliness of the crowd. In some ways it is possible to be more lonely in an airport, or even in a big sanctuary, than in one's own room. Good as solitude sometimes is, each human being requires, for his own best development, some connection in which loneliness is transcended by genuine sharing. This will not come by some psychological trick, or by training, which is merely that of "sensitivity," but it can come by a mutual commitment to the same ends and by helping one another in a common task. When the students and the professor lay a brick walk together, talking, as they work, about their deepest convictions, they realize, after the task has been completed, that their experience has provided an alternative to loneliness. There is fellowship which is produced by worship and there is fellowship which is produced by work, but the best fellowship comes from the combination of the two.

The development of groups which meet some of the requirements just delineated will help to liberate the unused powers of the various persons mentioned in Chapter II, particularly women and youth. Women in the ordinary church are already members of various "circles," but too often these are largely social in orientation. Great energy is expended on the conduct of teas and on bazaars. Even though the money produced by bazaars may do good, the latent power in Christian women is not normally liberated in this fashion. The liberation will not come, in most lives, unless there is more stimulus to think and to share at a deep level. Furthermore, the service is more valuable if it comes directly rather than by proxy, in the provision of financial support to others who serve.

It is hard to think of a way in which, in his present mood,

the characteristic young person of college age can be expected to enjoy participation in the public worship of either the ordinary church or the radical sect. The former seems to him irrelevant and unproductive, while the latter seems to him to be culturally impoverished, in spite of its evident vitality. The failure of the sects to engage in intellectual self-criticism causes them to lose the children of their members almost, though not quite, as much as occurs among the more respectable congregations. Here, then, is the manifest opportunity in both camps for a new approach.

What kind of religious life is possible in today's colleges? Many who feel the problem most deeply now wring their hands in despair. The required chapel has been largely given up, though usually for the wrong reasons, and often in a mood of abdication. The voluntary chapel sounds fine in the catalogue, but it sometimes amounts to practically nothing. The numbers of those who attend may equal those of a small group, but, because the small group mentality is lacking, the spiritual and moral effects are slight. While a few gathered in a circle in a small room may be powerful, a few scattered in a large place of worship are merely pathetic.

The decline of old patterns leaves room for the emergence of new ones. But, unless we are careful, the new patterns may be as disappointing as are the old, though for different reasons. In some academic communities there is a religious program, which is limited almost entirely to social action, to tutoring slum children, and to political propaganda, without any attempt to support all of this by prayer, worship, and study of the life of Christ. Consequently, the program has the appearance of vitality, but it is actually short-lived and sometimes encourages the exact antithesis of a loving spirit.

The band pattern would seem to be ideally suited to

those who are truly seeking an alternative to both superficial piety and superficial activity. A recent letter from a student in one of the most prestigious of the colleges for women expresses the need succinctly. What she feels very keenly is the need for the production of a group of Christian intellectuals frankly devoted to the penetration of the humanistic and naturalistic walls which surround every contemporary student. "I am," she writes, "nineteen and a sophomore. As a Christian I am disturbed by the lack of academicians within the Church (to whom I can turn for spiritual help), and the almost direct refusal to recognize a place for 'intellectualism' within the fellowship of believers. I often feel that I am expected to drop my 'book learning' as I walk through the doors of a church building, as if facts and faith were mutually exclusive. I get no sound encouragement in this area of my life from Christians, and I feel that I need the help, because I have a peculiar mission-field to some of today's 'young intellectuals' as I show them how the Lord makes each day an adventure in living. As a young person and a follower of the Way, I often feel almost forsaken by the older Christians in any attempts to witness to my peers. I am excited and willing to *act.*"

As the reader is probably able to conclude, letters like this constitute one of the major rewards that come to an author. Furthermore, correspondence on this level is a learning process for both parties. What is most remarkable about the thinking of this young woman is that she envisages her own mission field so distinctly. She is wise enough to realize that her own academic community is the very place where she is needed. The strong probability is that most of her fellow students, and also her professors, have not even entertained the idea that it is possible to combine genuine reverence with intellectual integrity. Operating upon the unargued, and therefore unexamined, assumption that reverence and integrity are incompatibles, between which it is necessary to choose, the majority of the best minds naturally rejects the former in favor of the latter. What a chance this virgin field presents to young people who are ready to learn from all who can provide help, including one another, about the best ways of presenting an examined faith persuasively.

Here is the perfect setup for a contemporary volunteer band. There is a clear need for directional fellowship, for prayer and for study, but these must not be sought as ends in themselves, valuable as they are. All are introduced for a concrete purpose, the purpose of creating a missionary band in contemporary Academia. Such a group is magnificently self-justifying. All of the discipline, all of the study, all of the silence are required for an intelligible purpose. This purpose is fully in line with Basic Christianity, which teaches that men and women must seek to share whatever they really prize.

The cadre is one possible successor to the Student Volunteer Movement which was able to generate tremendous enthusiasm a half century ago, and in the entire period up to the Great Depression. The Student Volunteer Movement drew 8,000 young people to a convention in Des Moines in early January, 1920. Nearly all who attended this gathering planned seriously to give their lives to the missionary cause, presumably in foreign lands. These idealistic young people had heard Robert E. Speer say, "Any man who has a religion is bound to do one of two things with it, change it or spread it. If it isn't true, he must give it up. If it is true, he must give it away."

It is obvious to almost any observer that the steam has gone out of the foreign missionary movement and has indeed been gone for some time.[6] But this does not invalidate the potent idea; all that needs changing is the location

6. The exception to this is to be found in some Fundamentalist groups in which the sacrificial giving is as great as ever.

of the field. That the foreign service idea is valid and appealing is shown by the early success of the Peace Corps, though this particular effort appears to have passed its peak. Perhaps the Peace Corps was bound to be temporary, because it could be entered without depth of commitment. While the appeals of world travel and general human betterment may provide a certain level of motivation, they cannot, in the long run, match the motivation which, starting with the love of Christ, makes a person become a Brother's Brother or a Sister's Sister. Far from being obsolete, the missionary motive simply needs redirection and relocation.

The band of Christian intellectuals, though its most fertile field is the university community, need not be limited to such an area. After all, people do not live in Academia very long, and what is needed is something to which people can give their entire lives. Bands of Christian intellectuals, dedicated to getting their own minds clear in order to bring clarity to other minds, may reasonably be set up in ordinary towns, often within the fellowship of the Church. The enduring inspiration for this development of new Christian units is Christ's call for such a task force. It was because the people were confused, uprooted, and perplexed that Christ called for workers in the human harvest. Now, as then, there is not the slightest doubt about the need; the doubt is whether there will emerge enough people who will become part of the answer to the prayer for a labor force (Matt. 9:38 and Luke 10:2). What is sure is that the urgent need cannot be met by people working in isolation. Unless there is a band or something like it, not much will be accomplished.

We have been concerned, and rightly so, with physical hunger in the modern world and we are dedicated to its elimination. The probability that this can actually be accomplished arises from the important fact that many farmers can now produce 160 bushels of corn per acre. But a far more baffling problem is that of spiritual hunger. Most of our neighbors, while physically well fed or even overfed, are undernourished at another level of their experience. Millions do not believe anything or, if they do, they are very unclear about what it is. The most effective of all emerging Christian units in our generation may be those consciously conceived to meet this particular need. In the words of Cardinal Newman, the task of the bands which must be called into being is "to employ Reason in the things of Faith."

It is strange, when a new kind of Christian evangelism is so obviously called for, that we pay so little attention to Christ's own method. What we see operating, as we study the Gospels, is a band, often mobile in character, though not always so. At the beginning of the public effort, Christ recruited, not just admirers or worshipers, nor even supporters, but members of a task force. Sometimes we find all of them, both men and women, moving together from town to town (Luke 8:1-3). There was a constant mingling of both service to the people and instruction in principles. A very large part of the Gospels is given over to a report of activity and training of this small group gathered for a specific purpose.

If we are wise, we shall pay close attention, not only to the strategy of the band as Christ developed it, but also to His practice of employing a smaller unit of only two members. The most striking illustration of this strategy is the sending out of the Seventy (Luke 10:1 ff.). Seventy was apparently a number too large for efficient operation, but the alternative was not operation one by one; it was the use of teams of two. What is especially noteworthy about this particular stratagem is its signal success which astounded even the participants. "The seventy returned with joy, saying, 'Lord, even the demons are subject to us in your name!' " (Luke 10:17). It is wholly possible for a man to pray alone or to meditate alone, but the lone penetration of alien territory is not likely to be effective. That the territory was truly alien Christ left no doubt, even saying that the little teams were "lambs among wolves" (Luke 10:3, NEB).

The use of teams of two among the Seventy reflected what had already been practiced among the Twelve. After the sorrowful and disappointing experience at Nazareth, when Jesus left the synagogue which He seemed to consider henceforth as a barren fig tree, He started the strategy of commissioning teams of two, drawn from the band. "And he called to him the twelve," reports Mark, "and began to send them out two by two, and gave them authority over the unclean spirits" (Mark 6:7). The careful reader will note that, in both Matthew and Luke, the names of the Twelve Apostles are listed in pairs (Matt. 10:2, 3 and Luke 6:14-16).

A contemporary band of Christian intellectuals will need frequent reminders similar to those found in the Gospels. They will, for one thing, need to remember that their reception will often be unfriendly. As they try to help others, and especially their peers, to find an intelligent faith which will give stability to their lives, they must expect a steady barrage of criticism. They must be prepared to hear quotations from Sigmund Freud, particularly from *The Future of an Illusion,* and they must expect many revised versions of the claim of Karl Marx that religion is the opiate of the people. They must learn to bear the condescension of professors and the violent antipathy of the New Left, which supposes that it has a monopoly upon crusading zeal. A group dedicated to the promotion and intellectual defense of Basic Christianity is engaged in one of the most thrilling of enterprises, but it is also one of the most difficult tasks that can be imagined.

The way in which a band of intellectuals is recruited is a matter of the first importance. Certainly it cannot be formed by a public announcement or by advertising. We must be far more subtle than that. The only possibility of successful formation is that which necessitates individual solicitation. Watch for evidence of concern on the central subject, a concern which may be revealed by letters or by casual conversation, as well as by the direct report of desire to be engaged. The whole operation is spoiled if the standards are lowered in order to include those who are unwilling to accept soldierly discipline or who want all of their thinking to be done for them by others.

If we inaugurate new societies of Christian intellectuals, we must also be prepared to nourish them. This responsibility requires the establishment of new centers of training and encouragement which can operate in our time as St. Columba's base operated on the Island of Iona when the Christianization of Scotland was seriously attempted nearly fourteen hundred years ago. Whether the existing theological seminaries are sufficiently flexible to serve in this capacity we do not know. The probability, however, is that we shall have to establish training centers of a radically new and highly imaginative character. These will be centers which link the tenderness of the warm heart with the humility of prayer and a tough-minded rationality greater than we have normally expected.

The worst nightmare is not the disappearance of Christianity, but its continued existence on a low level. This is what may occur, for a while, unless a more demanding rationality emerges in the Church of Christ. The story of Christian history includes, we must admit, frequent decline, as well as advance. Because there is no known insurance against loss of devotion, this may occur even to the contemporary bands, but the good news is that, when old Christian societies die, others can arise to accept the responsibility of attack upon the world. This is how the Church of Christ operates.

IV

THE NEW EVANGELICALISM

*Hold to Christ, and for the rest be totally un-
committed.*

HERBERT BUTTERFIELD

THE MOST instructive single feature of contemporary student unrest is the evidence it provides that
thousands are looking for something to which they can
give their lives. Herein lies an almost unparalleled opportunity for those who have found, in their experience, a
depth of meaning which they can share. Part of the challenge arises because we live in an age which, in its pervasive anti-intellectualism, is largely ignorant of theology.
The rational basis for belief in God is not antiquated, for
the simple reason that most people have never heard it
presented. To our sorrow, it is the practice of many religious leaders, including pastors, to avoid the central questions of faith. The avoidance of theology has been more
harmful than we usually realize. The damaging conse-

quences, far from being limited to the spiritual poverty of the lone individual, are exhibited in society.

A vivid example of social harm arising from theological ignorance is that of the reaction which often follows uncritical idealism. Much of the bitterness which produces violent destruction of life and property is exhibited by those who have grown up expecting everything to be ideal, if only people are willing to work at the job of human betterment. When experience finally teaches that this sentimental view of reality is false, many, feeling betrayed, lash out with denunciation in every direction. If poverty cannot be eliminated in two years, the government must be to blame!

In the beginning, in our generation, we tend to start life with a beautiful vision of all schools integrated, all streams unpolluted, all wars eliminated. The unchallenged assumption is that of the possibility of instant Utopia, because we suppose that the barriers to it are external forces. The Utopian crusader is vulnerable to frustration precisely because he does not know what even the simplest Christian believer knows, namely, that the chief hindrances to an earthly paradise are internal ones.

An understanding of the Christian doctrine of sin and its pervasiveness might do wonders in the modern world. It would, in any case, liberate us from the assumption that all corruption is produced by external causes. It is obvious that exclusive reference to external factors takes away any rational basis of responsibility, and that, apart from the reality of responsibility, no moral order is possible. But the best thing which the doctrine of sin can do is to help the moral crusader to realize that sin can enter *even into his own crusading.* A sound theology makes it clear that corruption is pervasive in the human race, appearing among the learned as it appears among the ignorant, and among the professionally religious as among lay men and women. It is no respecter of persons! The classic Christian faith is thus the exact antithesis of all idealism which is based upon belief in innate human goodness, the false assumption that all men would be kind and good if only they were not corrupted by "society."

The recovery of the doctrine of sin has been made possible by a number of distinguished Christian intellectuals in our century among the most eminent of these being T. S. Eliot and Reinhold Niebuhr. The enduring effect of Dr. Niebuhr's teaching lies at this point and is given its fullest expression in his Gifford Lectures, *The Nature and Destiny of Man.* The essence of sin, in Niebuhr's teaching, is "inordinate self love."[1] It is not merely "the drag of man's animal nature," and it is not just the corruption produced by environmental factors.

The doctrine of sin is not only the most empirical, but also the most sophisticated of all Christian doctrines. It is sophisticated in that it refuses to settle for simplistic views of human life. It is compatible with emphasis upon the universal possibility of renewal because, though all men are sinners, all men, at the same time, are bombarded by the love of God. The Living Christ stands at every human door and knocks (Rev. 3:20). God has not left any one of His children without a witness (Acts 14:17). To stress the universal witness, without reference to the ubiquity of sin, is to be unrealistic; to stress the reality of sin, without the divine initiative, is to surrender to despair. "The Christian religion, then," said Blaise Pascal, "teaches men these two truths: that there is a God whom men can know, and that there is a corruption in their nature which renders them unworthy of Him."[2]

It is widely recognized that no one has equaled Blaise Pascal in his vivid understanding of both the greatness and

1. New York: Charles Scribner's Sons, 1941, Vol. I, p. 252.
2. *Pensées,* 555. The numbering follows that of Leon Brunschvicg.

the littleness of man. What is sorrowful, says Pascal, is that man is a sinner; what is glorious is that he can know it. "For in fact, if man had never been corrupt, he would enjoy in his innocence both truth and happiness with assurance; and if man had always been corrupt, he would have no idea of truth or bliss."[3] People who understand this combination do not give up, and they try to leave the world relatively better than they find it, but they have a built-in antidote to moral shock in that they are prepared to resist the bland optimism which sometimes characterized the early social gospel. They are skeptical of all schemes for the rapid overcoming of social evils since they are aware that human beings, particularly in their group life, are inevitably caught up in the clash of self-interest.

One of the most frightening historical developments of this century was the growth of the Hitler Movement, with the channeling of idealism into a pattern of violent denunciation. What we need to realize is that much of this tragedy can be repeated, and that it *will* be repeated unless we have an improvement in our own philosophy. One of the signal contributions which a band of Christian intellectuals might make would be in the avoidance of the calamity which comes when idealism turns sour. This is a good illustration of how the Christian faith exists, not merely for the sake of the individuals who espouse it, but for the sake of the world.

If we are to have, not a perfect society, but a relatively better society, we must give careful attention to the problem of belief. People without a sound theology are bound to have a poor one, for theological questions are intrinsically unavoidable. Beliefs are important, partly because they determine, in large measure, what men do. By belief in a proposition we mean the determination to act as a man *would* act, if he knew that it were true. In short, belief

3. Ibid., 434.

involves, not merely abstract reasoning, but the response of the whole person. Since the test of the genuineness of a belief is practice, propositions in the Christian system are all of the nature of requirements to action. What do we do when we examine the proposition: God is? We see at once, if we are precise in our analysis, that it is either true or false. If it is false, we should forget it. If it is true, we should act upon it. The one thing which the tough-minded Christian soon realizes that he cannot do is to assent to the proposition and then do nothing about it. That, indeed, would be the mark of an unstable mind. Men cannot accept Christ and leave the matter at that unfinished point. If He tells the truth, men must follow Him!

This is not the place to explain in detail why belief in God, as the Creator and Sustainer of the universe, makes sense. It is right to say here only that those who dismiss the reality of God lightly are illustrating a dogmatism that has no intellectual justification. Those who declare, as many do loudly, that the theism which Judaism, Christianity, and Islam have in common is incapable of logical defense, are merely revealing their failure to come to grips with some of the best thinking of the world.

There are many reasons for supposing that the dogmatic atheist is wrong, but, for the thinking layman, the most persuasive method is that of emphasis upon converging lines of evidence. Cumulative evidence is what all of us find persuasive when we are dealing with the facts of history, as in the case of a crime, with several lines pointing in the same direction. Evidence is multiplied when it is added! The evidence that this is God's world, rather than a meaningless accident, is of this nature. We see something of the logical convergence when we note that, on the one hand, we have general theistic conclusions which the study of philosophy provides, while, on the other hand, we have the remarkable reports of direct religious experience on the part of people who testify, generation after generation, that God has reached their lives. While each of these lines of evidence is impressive alone, the combination is something so strong that it would require unusual arrogance to ignore it. It is important to realize that many modest individuals are entirely able to share in the empirical evidence when they could not possibly engage in the philosophical approach. The unpretentious man who says, "I know God *is,* because He spoke to me this morning," is really a member of a noble fellowship, which may be termed the "fellowship of verification." This fellowship includes, not only a host of plain people, but intellectual giants of the character of Blaise Pascal. The famous French thinker would never have written the *Pensées* had he not experienced a direct encounter with the Living God which dissipated his doubts and altered his career. If he, or any other reporter of the encounter, is trustworthy and undeluded, we cannot avoid the logical conclusion that God really is.

Though this line of thinking is both sound and persuasive, the Christian has another, which brings powerful additional support. This arises from the undoubted fact that Christ *believed.* A Christian is one who, in spite of his sins and failures, has become convinced that he has found one solid place in his total world, a place from which he can operate with confidence, the trustworthiness of Christ being the basic and primitive proposition in his system of values. He is thus committed, but his is not a blind faith, because, as he examines his world, this makes more sense than does any other alternative basis of trust of which he is aware. Furthermore, as he proceeds experimentally, his fundamental basis works in practice. Always it is a gamble, but it is not a wild one.

Now the point which the thoughtful Christian is forced to make is that the conviction of the trustworthiness of

Christ leads inevitably to the conviction that the Living God really *is,* and that He is profoundly personal. Otherwise Christ's use of "Thou" is unjustifiable. The Christian whose faith is threatened can do no better than to return, again and again, to the brief prayer from the lips of Christ which appears in two of the Gospels: "I thank thee, Father, Lord of heaven and earth, that thou hast hidden these things from the wise and understanding and revealed them to babes" (Matt. 11:25 and Luke 10:21). Either God really is and is One with whom we can converse, or Christ was wrong, and wrong at the deepest point of His conviction. A Christian is, among other things, one who believes that Christ was right and continues to be right.

Once we have seen both the importance and the necessity of belief, we must go on to ask what the particular character of the belief ought to be. This is an inquiry which must never come to an end because we are always operating within the limitations of human finitude. It is the recognition of intrinsic human limitations that makes all dogmatism inappropriate. But, though we are denied the luxury of absolute certainty in our beliefs about anything, with the consequence that we are forced to live by faith, some items of faith are far more dependable than are others. Our task is to learn from experience and to draw rational conclusions from what we are able to observe.

To some Christians it appears that the major choices of Christian belief are limited to Fundamentalism and Liberalism. By Fundamentalism is meant a position which its upholders suppose is identical with historic orthodoxy, though often this is not the case. We do not, of course, hear the word Fundamentalism very much today, the word having gone out of fashion, but large numbers still adhere to what the term once denoted. The major mark of this position is strict literalism about the Holy Scriptures. Reacting, understandably, against the superficiality of religion in general, people recognize that they need something firm and this, they assert, is found in an unabashed Biblicism. Adherence is given to any doctrine, if the Bible supposedly teaches it.

The position just mentioned has relatively little support among the most influential religious leaders, but it is still the position of millions of people who have few able spokesmen. Part of the sadness of the religious scene is that there is often no real communication between masses of modest Christians and the ecumenical leaders, who are more truly isolated than they realize.

The major difficulty of Fundamentalism, by whatever name, is its inability to give an intelligible account of the Christian faith. Seldom does it indicate clearly how it is possible to be a sincere Christian and also to accept the major conclusions of natural science. It is not necessary to adopt scientism, or the idolatry of science, to understand that science is here to stay. The combination of science and technology, which made possible the landing of men on the moon, is something which every reverent man is bound to honor. Somehow, if we are to live intelligently, we must find a way to hold, without incompatibility, reverence for the Creator and also the major findings of geology and the other sciences. The unfortunate fact is that this is something which the strict Biblicist cannot do.

Though many proclaim their Biblical literalism with confidence, it is soon evident, when we make careful inquiry, that the alleged literalism is actually held with reservations or with ambiguity. In practice, people choose which passages they elect to take literally, and which ones they elect to interpret metaphorically. It seems impossible, for example, to find anyone, in spite of his protestations, who interprets baptism by fire in a nonfigurative fashion. A good example of the problem which the literalist faces is that presented by the words of the Apostle Paul when he is definite on a number of subjects, such as the superiority of the unmarried state (I Cor. 7:7), and the subordination of women. How many are there, in fact, who accept without qualifications the assertion that, if there is anything women desire to know, "let them ask their husbands at home" (I Cor. 14:35)? If the literalist dismisses this unambiguous imperative by saying that it applied only to a particular situation, where there was a special problem of overtalkative women, he has already undermined his own general position.

Much as we may admire the sincere devotion and sacrificial giving of many persons in the Fundamentalist camp, we must conclude that theirs is not a live option in the contemporary world. The Christian does not dare to take a stand which he cannot accept with the concurrence of all of his mental powers. We do not know very much, but we at least know that we must avoid obscurantism. The Christian faith is disloyal to its own genius whenever it undertakes to prevent enlightenment.

In the thinking of many persons, the only alternative to Fundamentalism is some form of Liberalism. Because, by the very nature of the case, Liberalism is a varied phenomenon, it is harder to describe than is Fundamentalism, but the general form is recognizable. Liberalism is marked, for the most part, not by what is believed, but by what is not believed. For example, one who labels himself a liberal Christian may not believe in the inerrancy of the Scriptures, in the virgin birth, in the bodily resurrection of Christ, or in the Second Coming of Christ. The spectrum of Liberalism is so wide, however, that it may include many more negations than those just mentioned, some of which are far more extreme. Thus it is not uncommon to find clergymen who reject the possibility of miracles or of the resurrection of Christ.

The chief way in which all Liberalism is vulnerable is

that it is inherently ambiguous. As a mood of openness to new truth from whatever quarter, it is unassailable, and must therefore be part of any honest approach to the truth. If a liberal is one who draws his conclusions upon the basis of evidence and is ready to change when new light appears, then it follows that every person of intellectual integrity is a liberal. But the situation is entirely different if we are talking about a creed. Some assert that the one positive feature of the liberal faith is the dignity of man, but this only raises new questions. Anyone with a philosophical bent is aware that the doctrine of human worth is one which cannot stand alone, all of its validity being derivative.

One apparent item of liberal belief is *freedom,* but the trouble is that this may mean anything. "The world," said Lincoln, "has never had a good definition of the word liberty." Complete freedom is complete nonsense, because it includes the right to deny freedom to other people. When anyone says that he believes in freedom, we have no means of knowing whether he refers to *freedom to* or merely *freedom from.* If he means the latter, there is no positive content in his faith, while, if he means the former, he is valuing something else above freedom, and this is determinative of his conduct.

Ambiguous as the liberal creed may be, it is only fair to point out that many Christians, who espouse the liberal cause, are obviously sincere and have a valuable contribution to make. Even their negativity is a reaction to something which seems to them evil. Many of these have been touched by the spirit of Christ and they are trying, consequently, to relate to the contemporary needs of perplexed men and women. As we observe the Christian scene, we recognize that persons tend to classify themselves as liberals, not because they actually have a liberal creed, but because they are in honorable revolt against close-mindedness. Liberalism, at its best, is therefore a matter of mood.

It is a striking fact that, for the most part, the greatest decline in Christian vitality is shown today by those groups which pride themselves upon their Liberalism and upon little else. This is not really surprising, since people will dedicate their lives only to something that is positive. People are not held together very long by a consideration of what they do not believe. Note that the erosion of faith, which caught public attention for a brief period when "Christian atheism" was seriously proposed, was the logical result of certain liberal tendencies. Once the first step of denying that God is a Person has been taken, there is not much to keep people from moving further in the same direction until they deny God completely.

Fortunately, an antiquated Fundamentalism and a largely sterile Liberalism do not exhaust the practical possibilities of the Christian Cause. One of the most heartening facts of our particular time is that a genuine third option is coming into being. The third option, which is developing with impressive speed, may best be termed the New Evangelicalism. Justification of this terminology is possible in reference both to the noun and the adjective. One new development is the fact that the proposed plan of union of nine Protestant denominations is unapologetically evangelical in emphasis. The Church which is envisaged for the future will, we are told, be *catholic, evangelical,* and *reformed.* By evangelical the authors of the plan mean "radically Christ-centered."[4]

"Evangelical" is the only Christian adjective which is better than "catholic." All of us, if we are sincere, try to be catholic, knowing full well that Christ has other sheep which are not of our particular fold. But, in spite of this, we also know that no existent Church is truly catholic, for each is a fragment at best. The emphasis on universality is

4. *A Plan of Union* (Princeton: Consultation on Church Union, 1970), p. 20.

consequently a matter of hope, far more than it is a matter of experience. Whereas catholicity is valuable as part of the content of a dream, the evangelical faith, by contrast, is a fact of current experience. There are, as a matter of fact, great numbers of modest people who, in spite of personal failure, are really committed to a Christ-centered faith. They may, in addition, believe more than this, so that they divide on the edges, but they do not divide at the Center. More and more their golden text is "For I am not ashamed of the gospel: it is the power of God for salvation to every one who has faith" (Rom. 1:16). Evangelical Christianity, as we know it in experience, has many defects, but it is fundamentally hopeful because it exhibits a built-in capacity for renewal and redirection, which comes from contact with the Center.

The justification for the employment of the adjective "new" depends upon the recognition of three important current developments. In the first place, we see around us a new emphasis, among evangelicals, upon the necessity of being *rational.* This, of course, is not wholly new, but an increasing number of persons who are unashamedly Christ-centered are seeking, in fundamentally fresh ways, to profit from careful intellectual inquiry. A symptom of this is the recent decision of the publishers of *Christianity Today* to make available, for a wide reading public, five of the short books of C. S. Lewis in one large volume. The publication of *The Best of C. S. Lewis* is a significant service because it enables many readers to subject their minds, for the first time, to the powerful impact of the thinking of an undoubted rationalist. The response with which this has been welcomed is evidence that it is not inaccurate to refer to a growing body of Christian opinion called Rational Evangelicalism. One of the best things C. S. Lewis did, in his truly remarkable career, was to make readers critical of the absurd, though widely accepted, notion that the enemies of the gospel have a monopoly upon intellectual acumen. If he did nothing else, he turned the tables! The old Devil of the *Screwtape Letters* warned his nephew against letting people *think*. "The trouble about argument," he said, "is that it moves the whole struggle onto the Enemy's own ground."

The second perceptible mark of newness, in the evangelical faith, is that many of its adherents are becoming socially conscious. This change, which is obvious to any attender at conferences devoted to evangelism, is a sign of hope. If a person can start with a life-changing experience of the love of Christ in his heart, and can go on to try to overcome poverty and war, without, in the process, losing the dedication which originally motivated him, the result is a really powerful combination. One relevant item of evidence is found in the autobiographical essay "Reflections in Retrospect" by Frank E. Gaebelin, published by *Christianity Today* in its issue of July 31, 1970. "I am distressed," says this deeply committed Christian educator, "that it took me so long to realize that social concern is a vital biblical imperative." Among the recent gatherings, at which there has been evident a willingness to add the dimension of social concern to that of personal evangelism, was the conference at Wichita, Kansas, called in July, 1970, by the Friends Evangelical Alliance. In any case the persons who suppose that contemporary evangelicals are satisfied merely to stress individual salvation have not kept abreast of the times.

It is possible, of course, for the movement in the direction of wholeness to come from more than one side. It is encouraging to find avowed liberals, who heretofore have been limited to a merely activist program, now recognizing the necessity of the renewal of the inner life. Hopeful as this restoration of balance may be when it occurs, the move toward wholeness is much more likely to come from the other direction, as the evangelical, without losing his conviction, enters freely into social action.

The third evidence of novelty among evangelical Christians is the way in which they are ceasing to look upon themselves as an exclusive group. Many now admit that evangelical theology is weak whenever it becomes the exclusive spiritual property of one particular religious party. Some undoubtedly maintain the sectarian mood of supposing that those who are not marked by the evangelical name brand are not themselves evangelical, but the tide is turning radically against this manifest error. One form which the change is taking is the realization that evangelical commitment to Christ as the Center of Certitude is not the mark of a party, or even of a group of sects, but simply the central Christian emphasis in any generation. As soon as thoughtful people understand that evangelical theology is really *all that there is,* they already have an antidote to the creation of a group with a divisive label which finds its justification in the shortcomings of other Christians. Evangelicals, whatever they call themselves, are really disloyal to their own heritage if they are afraid of the full intellectual examination of their faith or are satisfied with a personal salvation omitting social consequences, or see themselves as an exclusive group. Fortunately, only a minority exhibits this disloyalty. It is increasingly common for contemporary evangelicals to understand that many in what they call the "liberal churches" are quite as Christ-centered as they are.

It is curious to see how evangelical theology has been ignored by those who have been able to dominate the ordinary media. Thus, in the very impressive and otherwise valuable issue of *Daedalus,* devoted to "Religion in America" (Winter, 1967), not one of the twelve contributors represents the position now under consideration. The closest approximation is that of the essay by William G.

McLaughlin, of Brown University, "Is There a Third Force in Christendom?" The chief focus of this valuable essay, however, is on the Pentecostal sects. These, indeed, demonstrate remarkable vitality, but few of them have made a serious contribution to evangelical thinking.

Whereas the Fundamentalism of a half-century ago undertook to defend several propositions, the Evangelicalism which provides a ground of hope in our generation proposes to defend only one. In the battle of ideas, the front has been strengthened, partly because it has been shortened. By means of logical implication, however, much else is involved because subsidiary items of faith follow necessarily from the primary postulate. For example, the Christian intellectual, who takes Christ seriously as his Center of conviction, is forced to include in his thinking a frankly supernatural view of reality. A person with a naturalistic bias normally doubts all reports of miracles, in the New Testament or anywhere else, not because there is a lack of historical evidence, but solely because miracle does not comport with his world view. He rejects the resurrection of Christ, not because it cannot be historically verified, but because he asserts, for some reason usually unexpressed, that such an event *cannot* occur. It is at this point that the evangelical Christian becomes the true skeptic and asks why such an event cannot occur. If he is forced to choose between a naturalistic dogma and the word of Christ, he chooses the latter, because he has more reason to trust a Person than a dogma.

It is obvious that, if Christ is dependable, the supernatural order of divine purpose is able to impinge, at any place or at any time, upon the natural order of events. If Christ is trustworthy, miracle is always possible, because the order of nature is subsidiary and is, in no sense, independent of God's continuing will. In one of his most arresting aphorisms Pascal wrote, "It is not possible to have a reasonable belief against miracles."[5] G. K. Chesterton supplemented Pascal's insight with his trenchant sentence, "The incredible thing about miracles is that they happen."

It is hard to see how a person can be a Christian at all and suppose that God is somehow denied direct access to His own creation, which we call the "natural order." The unlimited power of God is one of the most liberating ideas which a human mind can entertain, in that it sets a person free to look at any report with an open mind, without limiting preconceptions. If, for example, the changed lives of the Apostles makes the actual resurrection of Christ seem historically credible, we are free to believe in it. We are free to believe in it because this is God's world, and because He can make His purpose abundantly evident when the act of doing so accords with His will for the world and for men. The paradox is that, while the philosophical naturalist is bound, the Christian is free.

Because the creed of Naturalism has become the unexamined creed of millions in our generation, we must try to understand it. Probably no thinker of our generation has understood it better than did C. S. Lewis. "What the Naturalist believes," he wrote, "is that the ultimate Fact, the thing you can't go behind, is a vast process in space and time, which is going on of its own accord."[6] The chief reason why so many people reject, without further consideration, the twin ideas of miracle and a supernatural order is that they really believe that the natural order is all that there is. If events can be explained in a natural manner, there is clearly no need of explaining them in a supernatural manner.

It requires no deep thought to recognize that such a philosophy rules out prayer, in the sense of something which genuinely alters the course of events. But an evan-

5. *Pensées,* 814.
6. C. S. Lewis, *Miracles* (New York: The Macmillan Company, 1947), p. 16.

gelical Christian simply stands with Christ at this point. Christ not only taught the efficacy of prayer; He *engaged* in prayer, including prayer for others. Every effective prayer is a miracle, since it brings a new element into the causal series. The humble Christian, when he has to choose between orthodox naturalism and the teaching and practice of Christ, has no doubt where the weight of the evidence is. People are free to reject, if they wish, the whole conception of a supernatural order, but it is difficult to see why any honest man would claim to be a follower of Christ while doing so.

The New Evangelicalism owes a profound debt to such men as John Baillie and C. S. Lewis, who have done more than we ordinarily realize to set the tone of Christian experience, and to stiffen its intellectual structure. These men, widely recognized as giants, have helped mightily to show a way of avoiding submission to passing theological fashions. Often sincere Christians feel overwhelmed by what seems to be an academic consensus against them. On the basis of experience they have had reason to believe in the efficacy of prayer, but they doubt their own convictions because of the self-assurance of those who have dismissed their convictions cavalierly. Part of the current strength of the contemporary Christian intellectual is his new realization that his faith can hold its own in the market place of ideas. It is not the faith, but the hoary criticisms of the faith, which may be regarded as obsolete. The band of Christian intellectuals, which is now coming into being, is likely to grow in both strength and numbers. The person who is obsolete is the one who takes seriously the antique attack of men of the character of Lord Bertrand Russell. Christians may always be, in some sense, sheep among wolves, but they have strong contemporary defenders.

One step which is overdue in theology is the recovery of appreciation for William Temple. So faddish has been our recent theological education that many theological students of this particular generation have never read a word of Temple's great works, while others have not even heard his name, though he died as late as the period of World War II. In spite of changes of fashion, a good defense can be made for the judgment that Temple's *Nature, Man and God* is the most profound treatment of religious thought which has been produced in the twentieth century. The major secret of Temple's eminence was his wholeness. Though he was deeply devoted to social justice, he did not neglect the inner life of devotion. His two-volume work, *Readings in St. John's Gospel*, provides abundant evidence of the richness of his experience. It was said by a brilliant contemporary of Temple that, while *Readings in St. John's Gospel* was not the greatest book the Archbishop wrote, it was "the book of his that it took the greatest man to write."[7]

The Archbishop listened humbly to all that modern science could teach him, but he never succumbed to the seductive appeal of reductive naturalism. Though Temple was, in philosophy, a tough-minded realist, he was, at the same time, the most evangelical of Christians, in that the very heart of his experience was commitment to Christ. We know something of the superficiality of the recent past when we see a man of this character overshadowed by spiritual and intellectual lightweights.

When we try to describe the essence of the affirmative faith which can meet the needs of modern men and women, we find this to be an exciting and grateful task. We can be strengthened in this task by the recognition that what we are describing is not something strange, but the actual, though not fully expressed, faith of the majority of Christians in the modern as in the ancient world. They far

7. *William Temple's Teaching*, ed. by A. E. Baker (Philadelphia: The Westminster Press, 1951), p. 75.

outnumber those who, by their negative stance, get the headlines. It is helpful, in this connection, to remember that the most important events seldom or never get into the newspapers or on television newscasts. The very existence of a host of men and women who, in spite of their external differences, belong to the body of Christ, is news of the highest order of importance.

Because Basic Christianity is so widely misunderstood in the modern world, it is important to try to describe it. A Christian is a person who, though he knows that he is both ignorant and imperfect, believes that he has a clue to reality. He is not willing to settle for the notion that finite things and finite persons constitute the whole of reality, because he can see that they all point beyond themselves. In short, he *believes in God.* There is a radical difference between "believe in" and "believe that." The person who believes *in* involves his whole self in an attitude of trust.

The Basic Christian not only believes that God is, but he trusts Him, because he believes that God is like Jesus Christ. It is in this way that the Christian's faith is utterly specific. God might, of course, exist and yet be uncaring, and, if God is only an abstraction, this conclusion necessarily follows, since only persons care! The deepest conviction of the Basic Christian, however, is that the Center of Being is One who is like Christ. This is the only intelligible meaning of Christ's own claim to reveal the Father. At the heart of all reality there exists, then, not sheer power, but a Heart and Mind who notes even the fall of the sparrow (Luke 12:6). If this is true, it is the most revolutionary truth in the world. Accordingly, the central conviction of the Christian faith is best expressed, not by "the Divinity of Christ," but by "the Christlikeness of God." The Good News is that God exists, and is, in all eternity, what we see in Jesus Christ.

The doctrine of the Incarnation, which concerns the

most important single event in history, is not exhausted by reference to a Person who lived long ago in Palestine. The Hero of the story is God Himself! The Gospels are of transcendent value because of what they tell us of the eternal and unchanging nature of God. Since God is the Supreme Person, naturally His clearest revelation had to be, not in the starry heavens, wonderful and extensive as they undoubtedly are, but in a completely personal existence, with all its pains and victories. Christ is significant, then, in what He *reveals.* We encounter Him, as did the plain men and women of Galilee, or the Roman soldier, and suddenly it comes to us with a shock of revelation that this is what God is like. The nature of God, as depicted in Christ's words and deeds, was not something new, but something that has always been true. If there is any change, it is in *us,* and not in Him.

All else in Christian experience follows, by a divine dialectic, from this central conviction. If God exists, and if He is like Christ, the welfare of every finite person consists in conformity to His will. The effort to discover God's will for nations and for individuals is therefore a paramount undertaking. In this effort we never wholly succeed, but that is no reason for failing to try. Since we cannot expect to discover God's will alone, we need the help of other reverent seekers who make up the Church. This is why divine guidance need not be considered as something merely individual, though it may be individual and more. Science becomes significant because it is not only a way of manipulating events; it is above all a way of thinking God's thoughts after Him. Science is part of the Christian's task because it is a mental operation, and mind, if God really is, is the ruling principle of existence. Science may be valuable to religion preeminently by its ability to purge the believer's mind of illusion and superstition.

It is not really surprising that Evangelical Christianity

has exerted a pervasive influence upon education, especially in the formation and nurture of Christian colleges. If a man is to discharge his responsibilities in God's world, it is necessary for him to know as much as is possible, for true reverence never thrives upon ignorance. The Christian scholar will go as far as he can, in any particular science, convinced that knowledge is never a threat to his faith, but he will, at the same time, be sophisticated enough to realize that no law of nature, as discovered by physical science, is ever ultimate.

The Christian is concerned with social justice because he is concerned with men, the least worthy of whom may represent a greater wonder than any galaxy of stars. The connection between Evangelical Christianity and social service is far closer than is ordinarily supposed. The early nurture of antislavery conviction in strongly evangelical circles, such as that at Earlham Hall, Norwich, is a case in point, and it is not really surprising that this should be so. If God really cares for the sparrow, and if each impoverished or imprisoned human being is worth, in the Father's eyes, far more than any bird, it is incumbent upon reverent men and women to be God's agents in the world in order to enlarge the area of both love and justice. Faith is primarily a starting point, and from this starting point men, who understand what it is, are impelled to penetrate the world, whether it be the world of education, of scientific research, of government, or of social action. Christ's followers are called to share in the fellowship of penetration.

If God is like Christ, it would be illogical to assume that His concern for individual persons could come to an end with the death of mortal bodies. Consequently, firm conviction about the Life Everlasting is inevitably a part of any truly evangelical faith. Insofar as we trust in the Living God, we are bound to see Him as Lord, not only of the present, but of the future as well. To the rational being, it is an absurdity to suppose that the Lord of heaven and earth would, in the end, abandon those beings who, in spite of their sins, are the very jewels of His creation. If God is like Christ, it is a fair conclusion that personality will not end with our fleshly decay, but will continue and flourish in ways beyond our capacity either to ask or to think. It is not strange, therefore, that the last phrase of the Apostles' Creed is "And the Life Everlasting. Amen."

V

CIVIL RELIGION

Though with our limited understanding we may not be able to comprehend it yet we cannot but believe that he who made the world still governs it.

ABRAHAM LINCOLN

THE CHRISTIANITY of the future, like the Christianity of the past, will, if it is true to its fundamental genius, emphasize the Church as a gathered fellowship, but this does not mean that we shall be limited to this particular expression of religious vitality. While there is no possibility of Christianity without the Church, there can, in addition, be a valid Christianity *beyond* the Church. For many millions who have no real connection with the Church, and are not likely to have any, it will have to be the extra-ecclesiastical experiences that have meaning or none. Because the chief form which such experiences can take is that of civil religion, it is incumbent upon us to consider this aspect of religious life more carefully than we have done heretofore.

An essay of unusual intellectual and religious importance appeared in 1967, over the signature of Robert N. Bellah, Professor of Sociology at Harvard University. This important essay, called "Civil Religion in America," was originally published in *Daedalus* as first of the twelve articles on "Religion in America." Professor Bellah proposed to defend the thesis that "there actually exists alongside of and rather clearly differentiated from the churches an elaborate and well-institutionalized civil religion in America." The author succeeds in his ambitious effort. He shows that this religious dimension which, for the most part, has been either ridiculed or ignored, "has its own seriousness and integrity and requires the same care in understanding that any other religion does."[1]

There are many elements in the civil religion which American scholars are beginning to take seriously, the most obvious being those involved in inaugurations, in the celebration of Thanksgiving, and in Civil Rights marches. Though all modern nations have partial counterparts of these, a strong case can be made for the thesis that it is more in the religious sphere than anywhere else that the American culture can be seen as different from others which are similar economically and politically. Since we cannot escape history, a significant part of our culture arises from the fact that much of the founding, and much of the colonization to the west of the seaboard, was, for its participants, a deeply religious experience. We know something important about our country when we remem-

---

1. *Daedalus*, Winter, 1967, p. 1. The essay was subsequently published in *The Religious Situation: 1968*, ed. by Donald R. Cutler (Boston: Beacon Press, 1968). Though the important essay was republished without revision, except for the elimination of notes, its book form has the advantage of being followed by four responses, the authors of which are D. W. Brogan, Leo Pfeffer, John R. Whitney, and Phillip E. Hammond. Following these responses is Professor Bellah's own response, a commentary of significant value. The entire presentation occupies 63 pages. The essay is currently available in Robert Bellah's *Beyond Belief* (New York: Harper & Row, 1970).

ber that one of the most influential of its founders, William Penn, spoke reverently of his undertaking as "Holy Experiment in Government."

Religious scholars have been surprisingly slow to accept the fact that there is an elaborate system of practices and beliefs, born of America's historic experience and constituting the only real religion of millions of the citizens. It also bears mightily upon the lives of people who are members of churches and synagogues, though, in its major expression, it is free of association with any particular congregation or set of congregations. When Professor Bellah began to study this phenomenon, he was puzzled by the fact that anything so obvious should have escaped serious analytical attention.

The value of Bellah's religious thinking, in the judgment of fellow scholars, is indicated, in part, by the estimate of Phillip E. Hammond. "By its lucidity, its timeliness, its palpability," he writes, "Professor Bellah's essay stakes its own claim to greatness. . . . not until 'Civil Religion in America' was there a reasonably detailed and dispassionate portrait of this American 'theology.' For above all, Bellah takes seriously the idea of a national faith, locating its parameters without resorting to charges of syncretism and tracing its history as a parallel, rather than a substitute, religion in American society."[2]

Part of the reason for the neglect of civil religion is the strange development of the doctrine of separation of Church and State. To some this means bitter opposition to any religious overtones in anything connected with the government. In this extreme view, which is certainly not the view of the average citizen, it was wrong for an astronaut to read aloud from Genesis while he was circling near another celestial body. "In defending the doctrine of separation of church and state," Bellah says in a note, some

2. *The Religious Situation, 1968,* p. 381.

have "denied that the national polity has, intrinsically, anything to do with religion at all."[3] Much of the difficulty has also arisen from the peculiarly "Western" conception of religion as involving a single type of collectivity of such a character that membership is exclusive. There has been a curious failure to see that religious experience is of such potential magnitude that multiple memberships may exist without incompatibility. The more we think the more we realize that both the Church and the State may be valid means by which the divine leading may be known to men. There is nothing unreasonable about the belief that God can guide a nation as truly as He guides a Church. Here is one of the areas of experience in which "and" is a more profound conjunction than "or." If there are possible religious dimensions which we have partly missed, and which may enrich our lives in the coming days, we are foolish if we fail to try to see how to take advantage of them.

The first example of civil religion in the *Daedalus* article is that of the Inaugural Address of President John F. Kennedy on January 20, 1961. The fact that nobody was surprised by the religious overtones of this address is itself surprising. The concluding paragraph has already become part of our religious heritage, though the new President was not speaking for his own church or any other.

Finally, whether you are citizens of America or of the world, ask of us the same high standards of strength and sacrifice that we shall ask of you. With a good conscience our only sure reward, with history the final judge of our deeds, let us go forth to lead the land we love, asking His blessing and His help, but knowing that here on earth God's work must truly be our own.

There are many relevant comments to make about this eloquent statement. One of these is the degree to which

3. *Beyond Belief,* p. 187.

it is acceptable to great numbers of Americans, who would reply, if asked about their own lives, that they are not very religious. It is also worthy of note that such a devout expression can be made by the head of a great nation without embarrassment. Not even the probability that some cynic may say that an American President has to mention God if he does not want to lose subsequent votes, is a deterrent and has never been a deterrent since Abraham Lincoln set a new course in this regard. All Presidents since Lincoln have adopted his style, rather than that of his immediate predecessors, who normally made no forthright expression of their reverence even though, in several instances, it existed.

The people who dismiss the conclusion of the Kennedy address as only a ritual are likely to miss something of real profundity. America has not had since colonial days any Church establishment and is reasonably sure not to have any, so long as the Constitution stands, but this is by no means the end of the story. We have a vast amount of religion that is not Church religion and, however deeply we believe in the Church, we can be grateful that it is not all that we have. President Eisenhower was not a church member until after his election to the highest office, yet he went further than many of the others in this exalted position by actually giving his own inaugural prayer. And Abraham Lincoln who, by his example, made it seem normal to refer to prayer and to divine guidance, without personal embarrassment, never did join a church. We know something important about the civil religion of America when we realize the one President of whom there is a statue kneeling in prayer was never a member of a church anywhere. What is even more important to know is that this is not really a paradox.

It would be a serious mistake to jump to the conclusion that the civil religion, of which the inaugurations constitute one form of celebration, is merely the least common denominator of the "three major faiths." Naturally it draws on many of their sources, but it also has a character of its own. This character grows out of the peculiar historical experience of America interpreted, as Bellah says, "in the dimension of transcendence." Consequently it is not, in its noblest expressions, a watered-down version of either Christianity or Judaism.

Patriotism has long involved a religious dimension because of the obvious elements of dedication and sacrifice. We normally conclude that early Christianity represented a striking advance over the religions of Greece and Rome in that it included the Church, as the classic religions did not, but the truth of this conclusion does not mean that the classic religions were worthless. Even modern Shinto, comparable to Roman religion in many ways, has something to offer. Though Church and State are radically different from each other, there is no good reason to doubt that God can use both of them as instruments of His purpose.

There has been a tendency, among religious leaders of the recent past, to downgrade civil religion, speaking of it deprecatingly, but this may be a passing phase. After all, civil religion has been very important in world history. Who can doubt that Westminster Abbey, though radically different from a parish church building, has been a valuable asset to English life? That a coronation, there, is a religious experience for the British people is obvious. Fortunately, there is nothing wrong about the conjoining of the love of God with an exalted love of country.

America has no Established Church and no Westminster Abbey, but Americans have often been convinced that their entire national destiny is one which has a fundamentally religious character. The Lincoln Memorial in Washington is undeniably a temple. Christian congregations in which the people sing the fourth stanza of "America" may be sneered at by those who think expressions of patriotism are inappropriate in church life, but it is notable that the ones who do this are not less reverent and often show more vitality than do others. One would have to be really cynical not to be lifted by the experience of reverent people singing in unison:

> Our fathers' God, to thee,
> Author of liberty,
> To thee we sing;
> Long may our land be bright
> With freedom's holy light;
> Protect us by thy might,
> Great God, our King.

Because we need all of the help we can get in maintaining decent standards of behavior in the human family, we rejoice when reverence and patriotism can be combined. There is no absurdity about the conviction that God had a special purpose in bringing the American nation into being against conspicuous odds. The chances of failure in original colonization, in the endurance of a new type of government, and in the survival of subsequent periods, especially during the Civil War, were impressive, yet survival has occurred. The fact that a man of the stature of Lincoln arose at the very time when he was needed, and when lesser men would certainly have brought disaster, is a matter for wonderment, if no more. Fortunately, Lincoln's own keen sense of the divine destiny of the Union and of the role which he felt led to play in its preservation, has become one of the brightest features of the civil religion of America.

The expressions which Lincoln used, and which have become valued parts of our national heritage, would be totally inappropriate if the stand of the extreme advocates of separation of Church and State were accepted as correct. One of the most helpful parts of Professor Bellah's admirable essay is that in which he deals directly with this question. "Considering the separation of church and state," he asks, "how is a president justified in using the word God at all? The answer is that the separation of church and state has not denied the political realm a religious dimension. Although matters of personal religious belief, worship and association are considered to be strictly private affairs, there are, at the same time, certain common elements of religious orientation that the great majority of Americans share. These have played a crucial role in the development of American institutions and still provide a religious dimension for the whole fabric of American life, including the political sphere."[4]

The careful listener to President Kennedy's Inaugural Address was almost bound to note what was deliberately omitted. The President was a Christian, and specifically a Roman Catholic Christian, but to this no reference was made. Failure to mention did not mean failure to value. President Kennedy omitted all denominational references, not because denominations seemed to him unimportant, but because they were not pertinent to his task at the time, which was, in Bellah's words, "the religious legitimation of the highest political authority."[5]

Very deep in the American consciousness has been the idea of the "American Israel." As the people of ancient Israel were led through the wilderness, in order that they might settle a Promised Land, so the early Americans were led. It was necessary for them to cross stormy seas in uncomfortable sailing vessels, plagued by much sickness and hardship. It was not unknown for half of the passen-

4. *Beyond Belief,* p. 171.
5. Idem.

gers to die before the ship reached the western shore of the Atlantic Ocean. After Robert Barclay was appointed by the Proprietors of East Jersey as their nonresident Governor, he sent colonists from Scotland, but many of them, including his own youngest brother, died on the way. There is something particularly appropriate about the fact that the ship on which David Barclay died, and which left Aberdeen in August, 1685, was called *America.* The American story, while it was one of hardship and danger, was also one of hope. One element of hope was that many felt that they were being used as instruments of God's purpose.

The American Israel idea is implicit in the words of George Washington in the First Inaugural Address, given April 30, 1789. "No people," he said, "can be bound to acknowledge and adore the Invisible Hand which conducts the affairs of man more than those of the United States. Every step by which we have advanced to the character of an independent nation seems to have been distinguished by some token of providential agency." With Lincoln, the Israel theme became explicit when, in his Second Inaugural, he said, "I shall need, too, the favor of that Being in whose hands we are, who led our fathers, as Israel of old, from their native land and planted them in a country flowing with all the necessaries and comforts of life." It is very doubtful if the new republic could have come into being, and have been so well established that it has a continuity rare in the world, had it not been for the conviction of the founders that God had led a people to an unspoiled land in order to establish a social order that should, eventually, be a light unto the nations.

The physical separation from Europe was a factor in the development of America's self-image and, ultimately, her civil religion. Some scholars recognize the degree to which the long distance traveled was, to settlers, a conscious advantage. For example, Father Bruckberger reports that

"the settlers, far from lamenting this distance, always con-
gratulated themselves that it was there. They lived as
though on another planet, and this was their dearest
wish."[6] The fact that the new promised land was very
different from the place of bondage made the development
of a Messianic mentality easier. "There never was a generation," said Increase Mather in 1677, "that so perfectly
shake off the dust of Babylon." It was not really difficult for
the settlers to believe that they were a chosen people or,
at any rate, in Lincoln's brilliant phrase, an "almost chosen
people." "When they looked back on the Europe they had
left behind, they spoke of it with the bitter scorn of the
Hebrews for Egypt or for the bondage in Babylon."[7]

With this historical background in mind, it is easy to see
why so much of the civil religion of America has had an
Old Testament flavor. Until recently the stories of the
Hebrew Scriptures have been well known and often
quoted, not only in Jewish, but in Christian circles as well.
Though, for many decades, actual church membership was
less common in America than it has been in the recent
past, this does not mean that the Biblical record was consequently unfamiliar. In the religion which was largely civil
in nature, rather than denominational, the Bible was a
remarkable factor of unity.

Because the term "civil religion" was invented by Rousseau,[8] and because, in the French Revolution, an effort was
made to nurture deliberately a certain pattern of belief and
practice, it might be supposed that the French pattern
would have been a major influence in the development of
American civil religion, but this is not what occurred. One

6. R. L. Bruckberger, *Image of America,* translated by C. G. Paulding and
Vigilia Peterson (New York: The Viking Press, 1963), p. 12.

7. Ibid., p. 13.

8. J. J. Rousseau, *Social Contract,* Book IV, Chapter 8. Rousseau's own faith
was not widely different from that expressed by Benjamin Franklin in his *Au-
tobiography.*

striking difference was that the mood of the French Revolution was stridently anticlerical, whereas the American
experience has included very little of this. The most surprising single feature of the American pattern is that the
civil theology and the church theology developed along
parallel, rather than opposition, lines. Part of this was possible because, in America, the connection with the Biblical
roots was never severed, as it was so largely in France. In
both revolutionary France and revolutionary America
there was a conscious dedication to liberty, but in America
this dedication, fortunately, had a deeper rootage.

The conviction of being called to an unfinished task
must be understood if many of our accepted symbols are
to make sense. Only in the light of this conviction can we
understand the One Dollar Bill with its motto "In God We
Trust" and the unfinished pyramid underneath which are
the words "Novus Ordo Seclorum," indicative of a new
emerging order. Any person who grasps the depth of this
conviction can understand why a country, in which
Church and State are separated, opens Congress with
prayer, adds the words "under God" to the Pledge of
Allegiance to the Flag, and sets aside, by Presidential de-
cree, one day each year as a day of Thanksgiving to Almighty God. What great numbers of Americans have understood for decades is that the two apparent alternatives
of an established church and an irreligious secularism do
not exhaust the existential possibilities.

Even though inadequate attention has been given to the
phenomenon of civil religion, it has sometimes been mentioned, patronizingly, as "religion in general." The more
we analyze, the more we see how unfair this judgment is.
Of course most spokesmen for America's civil religion do
not mention Jesus Christ, but there is no good reason why
they should. Some people even concluded that Lincoln
was not a Christian because his public references to "the

Savior" were few. Civil religion has tended to be entirely specific in that it has referred concretely to national destiny. Each man in public life also has a private life in which he can be as denominational as he pleases, but there has long been a tacit agreement to the effect that, in his public role, the leader should speak for the whole nation and not merely for his own part of it.

There is, and ought to be, a clear division of function between the civil religion and Christianity, which is the faith of the largest segment of the population. The founding fathers were wise enough to see that, just as the churches ought not to control the state, so the state ought not to control the churches. Accordingly, great latitude was granted, usually including freedom from taxation. In the thinking of Franklin and other early exponents of civil religion, it was not a substitute for the religion nurtured by the churches; they simply existed side by side.

Like any good thing, American civil religion can be debased and even perverted. At its worst it becomes a form of boasting which identifies too easily the will of God with the "American way of life." We are foolish, however, if we permit our recognition of this danger to blind us to the magnitude of the central idea. In the experience of those most responsible for the character of the American civil religion there has been the exact opposite of boasting. The founders were humbled by the idea that God might have a special purpose for the nation, because they were keenly conscious of their own inadequacies. This was expressed with magnificent clarity by President Lincoln in his letter to Eliza Gurney, of September 4, 1864: "The purposes of the Almighty are perfect, and must prevail, though we erring mortals may fail to accurately perceive them in advance."[9] This is the authentic note which, though it is

9. *The Collected Works of Abraham Lincoln* (New Brunswick, N.J.: Rutgers University Press, 1953), Vol. VII, p. 535.

not always echoed in American civil religion, provides it with a standard.

There has been a strange failure to recognize Abraham Lincoln as a profound theologian. Part of the reason for this failure seems to be the strong though unargued assumption that theology is the exclusive domain of those who are closely associated with the churches. Usually this has been true, but some in our time, including Reinhold Niebuhr,[10] have recognized in Lincoln's thoughts about God and man and country a depth of theology which we neglect at our peril. The people who conclude that Lincoln had no theology because he had no church membership demonstrate by this judgment a failure to appreciate the existence of a religion which, though it is not in conflict with that of the Church, is different from it. To the intellectual structure of this parallel faith Abraham Lincoln is the greatest single contributor.

Lincoln's theological insights were expressed at many different points in his life, but preeminently at two. These were, first, the critical period when he made the agonizing and eminently dangerous step of issuing the Emancipation Proclamation, and, second, the time of the second inauguration, when peace was at last in view. The difficult experience of announcing the Emancipation came during the same supercharged autumn when President Lincoln was interviewed by, and joined in worship with, Eliza Gurney, the widow of Joseph John Gurney, the famous Master of Earlham Hall. What Lincoln said in Mrs. Gurney's presence is an indelible part of the civil religion of America. Lincoln's powerful message was given spontaneously out of the silence which followed Mrs. Gurney's short prayer. The President's final words are printed as the epigraph of

10. See William J. Wolf, *The Almost Chosen People* (Garden City, N.Y.: Doubleday & Company, Inc., 1959), and Reinhold Niebuhr, *The Irony of American History* (New York: Charles Scribner's Sons, 1952), pp. 171-73.

this chapter. The most revealing single sentence, however, is as follows: "In the very responsible position in which I happen to be placed, being a humble instrument in the hands of our Heavenly Father, as I am, and as we all are, to work out his great purposes, I have desired that all my works and acts may be according to his will, and that it may be so, I have sought his aid."[11]

Here is an authentic example of the "vision of greatness," without which, as Professor Whitehead taught us, moral education is impossible. Naturally, most of the civil religion which is expressed never reaches any such height, but attention to the standard is valuable, partly because it helps us to know when we fail to reach it. Essential to the civil theology that has developed are these ideas: (1) that God has a purpose, (2) that finite men are called to be His instruments in the fulfillment of His purpose, and (3) that the American people are called to a special vocation for the sake of the world. Lincoln is the preeminent spokesman for civil religion because he developed all three of these items in detail. So deep was this entire system of thought that it came out on some occasions without premeditation. The supreme example of this is that of the Gettysburg Address, to which on November 19, 1863, Lincoln added the words "under God," so that the phrase became, "that this nation, under God, shall have a new birth of freedom." The words "under God," which are not included in the first and second drafts of the address, were coined, for the first time, as the President spoke. Much as Lincoln loved his country, he was increasingly conscious that it is not ultimate, but always stands under judgment. The nation, great as it is, is not autonomous or really sovereign, but is responsible to higher demands. This is why the President

---

11. *Collected Works,* op. cit., Vol. V, p. 478. There is some uncertainty about the exact date of the meeting with Mrs. Gurney, but we know it came soon after the Emancipation Proclamation was made public.

could suggest in his 1864 letter to Eliza Gurney that there may be a radical distinction between our purposes and the purposes of Almighty God. Herein, if it is truly understood, lies an antidote to all self-righteousness. By great good fortune, the civil religion of America acknowledges as its supreme expression Lincoln's Second Inaugural, in which there is a specific warning against the idolatry of a nationalism which is too sure of itself. We can always be helped to remember that God's ways are not necessarily our ways when we ponder the sentence, "the Almighty has His own purposes."

We recognize that, in the contrast between church religion and civil religion, the superiority is not always on the side of the former. In fact, it is embarrassing to compare the utterances of Lincoln with those of some of the eminent clergymen of the period. Consider, for example, the words of Henry Ward Beecher, perhaps the most famous preacher of the period of the Civil War. When they are placed side by side with Lincoln's utterances we can hardly believe what we see. In reference to Lincoln, Beecher said, "Not a spark of genius has he; not an element of leadership. Not one particle of heroic enthusiasm."[12] It is wrong to conclude, of course, that Beecher was representative, but the fact that a prominent man could be so wrong in the cruelty of his judgment of another man may help contemporary men to be less sure of themselves.

The recognition that civil religion exists, and that it is a legitimate expression of the religious spirit, makes a great deal of difference to our ideas as we undertake to share in the guidance of the future. Even if church religion should decay, which it probably will not, there may always be another resource. The recognition of the existence and validity of civil religion makes the recent decisions of the

12. Carl Sandburg, *Abraham Lincoln, The War Years* (New York: Harcourt, Brace & World, Inc., 1939), Vol. I, p. 555.

Supreme Court about religion obsolete in many ways. The assumption underlying these decisions, though apparently unrecognized by the authors, is largely to the effect that religion, to be valid, must be church religion. If civil religion does, in fact, exist and if it is as much a part of our heritage as any church is, the controversial conclusion that the state must be neutral as regards religion is accordingly undermined.

It is when we consider seriously the institution of Thanksgiving, at the end of each November, that we begin to see the real character of civil religion in America. Though the individual church congregations are normally involved in the celebration, sometimes arranging inter-church gatherings, the occasion originates not in the Church, but in the state. A day has been set aside for this purpose by every President since Lincoln regularized the practice in 1863. Celebrations prior to 1863 were sporadic,[13] but they have not been sporadic since that time. The notion that the state must be neutral in regard to religion is radically inconsistent with this unbroken practice for more than a century. The institution of Thanksgiving may be neutral as between denominations, as it ought to be, but it is not, by any stretch of imagination, neutral as between reverence and irreverence.

Thanksgiving Day, in our modern sense, was inaugurated by President Lincoln's proclamation made October 3, 1863, referring to Thursday, November 27, 1863. In a magnificent gesture, which superseded anything done ear-

13. Lincoln participated in one non-Federal "Order for Day of Thanksgiving" which was celebrated November 28, 1861. The call was made, however, not by the President, but by "The Municipal authorities of Washington and George-town in this district." Notice was given by Lincoln only one day in advance. On April 10, 1862, Lincoln made a Proclamation of Thanksgiving, asking worshipers to render thanks "at their next weekly assemblages in their accustomed places of public worship," but this was very different from the tradition he finally established, as was the celebration held on Thursday, August 6, 1863, after the victory at Gettysburg.

lier and apparently conscious that he was pointing the nation in a new direction, Lincoln invited his "fellow citizens in every part of the United States, and also those who are at sea and those who are sojourning in foreign lands, to set apart and observe the last Thursday of November next, as a day of Thanksgiving and praise, to our beneficent Father who dwelleth in the Heavens." By fastening upon a Thursday the wise man was refusing to be identified merely with those who regularly gathered on either Sunday or Saturday. He was staking out a claim for civil as against denominational faith, in an action which seems to have been deliberate.

Much of the credit for the modern institution of a Federal Thanksgiving celebration belongs to Sara Josepha Hale, Editress, as she said, of the "Lady's Book." She requested on September 28, 1863, a few minutes of the President's "precious time." The unique feature of her proposal was not a call for thanksgiving, which had been made on various earlier occasions, but the suggestion "to have the *day of our annual Thanksgiving made a National and fixed Union Festival.*" The President accepted the novel idea and acted with great speed. In this decision, as in so many others, he had the cooperation of William H. Seward, Secretary of State. The continuation of this remarkable innovation has constituted one of the unique features of American culture.

It is unfortunate that the first Thanksgiving Proclamation referring to a "fixed Union Festival" is not better known, since it is a production of genuine nobility. "It has seemed to me fit and proper," said the President in reference to manifest blessings, "that they should be solemnly, reverently and gratefully acknowledged as with one heart and one voice by the whole American people." The people were asked to pray "and fervently implore the inter-position of the Almighty Hand to heal the wounds of the nation and to restore it as soon as may be consistent with the Divine purposes to the full enjoyment of peace, harmony, tranquility and Union."

It was a mark of the growth of Lincoln's mind, as he became the chief theologian of civil religion, that he did not, in the autumn of 1863, ask people to gather, as he had done on earlier occasions, in their "accustomed places of worship." Where they might choose to gather made no difference at all. Everything possible was done to transcend divisiveness. The same effort to achieve unity at the deepest level is revealed in Lincoln's second Federal Proclamation, again suggested by Sara Hale, which was issued October 20, 1864. On this occasion he called upon all his fellow citizens "wherever they may then be" to "reverently humble themselves" on the last Thursday of November. Again, as in 1863, there was no reference to established houses of worship. The people involved might also, of course, be members of churches, but it was not in that particular capacity that Lincoln called them to "offer up penitent and fervent prayers and supplications to the Great Disposer of events."

The future of religious experience will be greatly enriched if it becomes part of our national consciousness that, however much we may value pluralism, there is something besides pluralism. "Are we not," asks Professor Hammond, "the most heterogeneous and differentiated people on earth, but has not some unifying idea held us together during the times when we might easily have split asunder?" The sociologist answers his own question when he notes that very deep in our consciousness is the conviction that, like the chosen people of old, we are called to engage in a great undertaking, to give a "light unto all the nations."[14] Any thoughtful reader can see that this unifying conception is full of dangers, but the antidote to the dan-

14. *The Religious Situation,* op. cit., p. 382.

ger, which produces more humility than pride, is the civil theology which saves us from the idolatry of a nationalism which fails to recognize that it is under judgment. Without this theology, American nationalism might easily be insufferable!

Professor Hammond makes us see how much potential religion there is outside what we usually considered ecclesiastical boundaries, by his special reference to public education. "The one place," he says, "where more people, more often, for greater lengths of time are confronted with the nation's faith is in public schools. Has it not been free public education that largely turned waves of immigrants into American 'believers'? . . . And, as foreign observers have noticed, does not the high school dominate the community landscape in mainline America in much the same way that the Cathedral does in Europe?"[15] When we see the public school as the chief vehicle by which the unifying civil religion can be celebrated, we are on completely new ground. Many of the heated arguments of the past about religion in the schools are thereby terminated. These arguments got their heat chiefly from the assumption that, if there is religion in the schools, it has to be church religion.

In his response to his friendly critics Professor Bellah rises to a genuine height, particularly by reference to the paradox that there is "one central strand of the American civil religion which does not make the nation ultimate."[16] The words "under God," which have been added to the Pledge of Allegiance to the Flag, may be the most profound words of all. This, we can quickly see, is consistent with the major heritage of the Biblical faith, chiefly because it has actually been nurtured by it. The independent witness of the Church helps to emphasize this central point, and thus the Church contributes to civil religion. In

15. Ibid., pp. 382, 383.
16. Ibid., p. 392.

this manner church religion and civil religion do more than proceed on their independent ways; they can actually help each other. Each provides assistance to the other in constructing "a model of a self-revising society which is not ultimate in any finite form but always subject to higher demands and considerations."[17]

Anyone who sees the "self-revising" civil religion as a genuine sign of hope for the long pull inevitably places much of his confidence in the continuing influence of Abraham Lincoln, but it is important to realize that Lincoln has thousands and perhaps millions of colleagues in this holy task. It is to the vast number of humble colleagues that Professor Bellah refers when he says, in conclusion, that "the non-idolatrous strand of the civil religion which I documented chiefly in the words of a few thinkers and statesmen, notably Lincoln, is also deeply embedded at the homely level of everyday institutions." Though the future of our religious life cannot be predicted with accuracy by anyone, we can at least know that the number of persons engaged in the creation of the future is large. In that, in the dignity of the task, and in the trustworthiness of our ultimate Source lies our enduring hope. There is a great future for a people who really believe the words of Lincoln at Albany, as the darkness was gathering. "I still have confidence," he said, "that the Almighty, the Maker of the Universe will, through the instrumentality of this great and intelligent people, bring us through this as He has through all the other difficulties of our country." These words were verified before, and they will be verified again.

17. Ibid., p. 392.

71 72 73 10 9 8 7 6 5 4 3 2